The Parent's Guide to
Neuropsychology

The
Parent's
Guide to
NEUROPSYCHOLOGY

Nicholas S. Thaler, Ph.D.

ISBN: 978-1-5369-7382-2

I dedicate this book to Ren Dutt Thaler,
who every day provides me with *in vivo*
examples of child development.

Contents

Introduction

"Jeff is doing really well this year, but there are still some concerns." "We're not sure if Clara is working to the best of her ability." "Michael sometimes bothers the other kids during lessons and we're not sure if there is something going on. Have you thought about having him tested?"

Have you ever heard anything like the above about your child? Maybe it was at a parent-teacher conference. Or maybe another parent casually mentioned something to you as you were in line for pickup. Maybe you yourself always wondered if there was something holding your child back, only to have another adult confirm your worst fears. It can be frightening to hear that your child might be struggling in school. Questions emerge, like "Is this school the right fit for her?" "Are we doing something wrong?" "Is there something we can do to fix it?"

In these situations, school counselors, physicians, and other professionals will often recommend psychological testing. Or sometimes, they will refer to it is as "neuropsychological testing" or "psychoeducational testing." What exactly do these terms all mean? You might look it up online and see a list of professionals, or such a list might be provided directly to you. You see a list of names, all with impressive credentials, and you consider that testing might be a good step after all. But you are still not sure – or at the very least, you would like to know what you are getting yourself in to. The process can be costly. It can take up time away from school. Sometimes, it can raise anxiety in both the child and the parent in what the evaluation might say or not say. You might be concerned that your child will be labeled with a diagnosis, or that the results will reveal something that you can't fix.

If you are experiencing something like this, then this book is for you.

Maybe you have already completed the evaluation. The results are done and you have a (sometimes quite long) report in your hands. The report is full of numbers and jargon, phrases like "Jenny's executive functioning was above average across numerous domains, with the exception of weaknesses in cognitively flexibility (TMT B t-score = 40; 16th percentile) and working memory PASAT Trials1–4 t-score = 42; 21st percentile)" or perhaps even more confusingly, "John's attention was characterized by fluctuations with strengths in sustained attention (67th percentile), divided attention (89th percentile), but with weaknesses in focused attention (15th percentile)." There might be a diagnosis, such as a "specific learning disorder" or a "sensory processing disorder" with a list of recommendations. Sometimes these recommendations may really speak for you and your child, while other times they feel alien or inapplicable for your situation. You might have gone through the entire process and feel it was worth it, but you still have questions and there are still uncertainties.

If so, then this book is also for you.

The decision to undergo a neuropsychological assessment is a serious one, one that deserves thought and care. This book is set up into two distinct parts. The first half is written to help you decide on whether such an assessment is appropriate for your child. Chapters will provide background on the who, what, where, when, and why of neuropsychology, how a typical evaluation might proceed, detailed information about the components within the evaluation, and how a neuropsychologist serves as part of a broader team. The second half of this book provides background on some of the common diagnoses that may be ultimately identified, and maybe more importantly, detailed information on appropriate treatments and accommodations. If your child has just undergone an evaluation, then this second half might be of particular interest to you.

This book has been written with you, the parent, in mind - speaking to you directly as someone who would like more information about the lengthy and complex process that encompasses a neuropsychological evaluation. I hope you find this information useful in assisting you and your child in finding his or her best path in life.

PART I

PREPARING FOR AN EVALUATION

CHAPTER 1

The Five W's

Who are neuropsychologists? What do they do?
Where and when do they do it? Why are they used?
This chapter will provide answers to all these questions.

The Who

Neuropsychologists are doctoral-level professionals with either a doctorate of philosophy in psychology (Ph.D.) or a doctorate in psychology (Psy.D.). Neuropsychologists obtain their doctorate degree through 4-6 years of graduate school, typically in a clinical psychology program. They see patients, take courses, and conduct research. After graduate school, they are admitted to an internship where they primarily see patients for one year.

Upon completing internship, most neuropsychologists will secure additional training at the post-doctoral level. Typically, this is a two-year fellowship specifically tailored for neuropsychology training and incorporates additional clinical work and training. Upon completion of this fellowship, neuropsychologists become board eligible – in other words, they can apply for the American Board of

Clinical Neuropsychology (ABCN) board. Neuropsychologists with the letters ABPP-CN after their Ph.D. have successfully completed their board certification. That said, there are many neuropsychologists who are not board certified, including some who have been practicing for years. Even today, not all newly trained neuropsychologists are board certified – some because they see little need to do so, others because they have not had the time to start the process. By finding someone who meets the board eligible criteria, you will at least ensure that they meet the standards required to practice clinical neuropsychology (see footnote 1).

When choosing a neuropsychologist, other factors to consider include:

Reputation: Word of mouth is perhaps the most powerful way to obtain a reliable name. If another family worked with a practitioner with satisfactory results, this is a positive sign this practitioner can work with you as well.

Availability: Some practitioners are extremely busy and schedule patients months ahead. How responsive are they and how timely are they in returning emails and phone calls?

Cost: Assessment costs range widely, in part related to reputation and experience, but also keep in mind the services that are being offered. As described in the *what* section of this chapter, there are different report types and some might be more suitable for your child than others.

Insurance: Some practitioners take insurance, for which they are compensated less than for private cases. Because of this, insurance cases may offer briefer evaluations and reports than do private cases.

Location: Practitioners who work near your zip code will know relevant counselors, educational therapists, and other resources. They may have a closer relationship with your school.

Experience: Training does not end after fellowship. Practitioners who have been working for years will be more experienced. They may be more familiar with the problems your child has, and be more connected with the community. On the other hand, those just starting out might be more available and charge less.

Methods: No two neuropsychologists work alike. Some break up assessments over 2-3 days while others allow for one-day assessments. Some regularly schedule school visits while others do not. See how many days the assessment will take, where the neuropsychologist is willing to go, and who he or she is willing to speak with (e.g. teachers, other professionals). Find out how long their reports take to be written, how soon can feedback be scheduled, and if the neuropsychologist will remain available after the assessment for follow-up consultation.

Training: It's important that anyone who does a complete neuropsychological assessment be a doctoral-level practitioner, preferably board eligible if not board certified. However, there are other types of practitioners that offer services that might be appropriate for your child's needs and who are qualified to do some assessments.

Educational/School Psychologist: This is doctoral-level degree (Ph.D or Ed.D) that focuses on learning in the school environment. School psychologists conduct assessments, usually focused on identifying learning disabilities, and coordinate students' care in the school environment. Often, a school psychologist will conduct the initial testing of a child and refer out to a neuropsychologist if deemed necessary.

Clinical/Counseling Psychologist: Many clinical psychologists are general practitioners of psychology while others choose to specialize in areas such as behavioral health, pediatric medicine, or drug addiction. All psychologists are trained to provide assessments and therapy and some psychologists elect to conduct assessments of children. These assessments might not be as comprehensive as a neuropsychological assessment, but depending on the question being answered, they might suffice.

Child Psychiatrist: Psychiatrists are medically trained doctors and therefore can prescribe medication, which psychologists usually cannot. As medical doctors, they are often the first or second practitioner to work with a child dealing with the mental effects of a medical illness. They often refer to neuropsychologists when there is a question about cognition – for example in cases involving ADHD or learning disabilities.

Licensed Master's Degrees: There are several practitioners who are eligible to practice at the Master's level (that is, two-year post-bachelor's degree). Licensed clinical social workers (LCSW), licensed marriage and family therapists (LMFT), and licensed professional counselors (LPC) are all trained to provide therapeutic services to individuals and couples.. Those who specialize in children are qualified to see your child. A board-certified behavioral analyst (BCBA) is another master's level degree that has specialty training in the behavioral sciences. Many BCBA practitioners specialize in treating children with autistic spectrum disorders.

Typically, anyone who uses the title "psychologist" has a doctoral level degree. However, in the state of California, there is a master's level degree called "Licensed educational psychologist" (LEP). Something to keep in mind is that most government and educational agencies do not recognize diagnoses provided by a master's level practitioner. Therefore, if you are seeking a diagnosis for your child it is recommended that you establish the practitioner's credentials and ensure that he or she has the training equivalent to a doctorate (Ph.D., Psy.D. or Ed.D.).

Cautionary Groups: The above degrees are established degrees for mental health practice However, mental health has yet to establish the same level of training standards that medicine has. You would never encounter a nurse who refers to him or herself as a "doctor" and yet, the equivalent of this does unfortunately happen in the mental health world. I will describe groups that may warrant some caution in approaching, particularly if you know little about the individual's reputation.

First, be careful of individuals who call themselves "doctors" yet do not have a doctorate in a field that allows them to practice. There are known cases of individuals with Ph.Ds in primarily academic fields, such as biology, experimental psychology, or even English or philosophy, who then go on to obtain a master's degree that allows them to practice. By mixing their practicing degree with their Ph.D., they might refer to themselves as "Dr. Smith" or such. This is actually an unethical practice as the Ph.D. came from a non-licensable degree, although it can be difficult to catch. Make sure that their Ph.D. is in the field that they are practicing.

Second, while the term psychologist is generally a protected term that only doctoral-level professionals can use (LEP being a unique exception), the term therapist is not. Someone who has never been to college, or even graduated high school, can refer to themselves as a "therapist" or "counselor" or "life coach" at any time in their lives. They might even have degrees and certifications granted by "boards" that will print up a degree if you pay their fee. Please note that not all practitioners who choose this path are incompetent; simply that there was minimal oversight in ensuring their competency. I would be especially wary of individuals who conduct assessments without an advanced degree.

The What

What exactly goes into an evaluation? While no two neuropsychologists work alike, there are common methods that are shared. Neuropsychology always involves the assessment of brain functioning. Such assessments examine cognition, behavior, and emotional functioning. Most assessments begin with an interview with at least one primary guardian and involves taking a comprehensive history of the child. Along with the initial interview, follow-up interviews with other adults involved in the child's life, including teachers and professionals are often conducted. There are often behavior and emotional questionnaires that will be distributed to you and other adults. These questionnaires generally ask for your report on how the child is functioning in one or more areas.

After the first interview, testing usually begins. The tests are varied in presentation but generally come in pencil-and-paper form or are sometimes administered on the computer. Some are designed to mimic core academic tests of reading, writing, and mathematics while others are more abstract. Children might have to arrange blocks (either with their hands or using mental imagery), find patterns, define words, memorize lists or images, and engage in other puzzle-like activities. Many of these tests resemble games and can be fun for children. Testing is usually conducted between 1-4 sessions. The exact number of sessions and hours varies depending on the age of the child, the nature of the problem, the neuropsychologist's style, and the referral question, but the usual length is between 4 and 8 hours.

When all is said and done, you will have a report detailing the results of your child's evaluation. This report has a number of uses. Along with clarifying diagnoses and establishing treatment plans, reports can provide detailed insights on how your child processes information. Is he a visual learner? Does she learn quickly but respond impulsively to questions? Does he have significant testing anxiety that interferes with concentration? Does she process auditory information fine but does not use any strategies to remember that information? These are all questions that the report can address.

The report can also be shared with other professionals. In the public school setting, reports are often required to set up Individualized Education Programs (IEPs) and 504 plans. Independent schools often request reports to set up their own system of accommodations for the child. Reports can be submitted to testing centers to request extended time, additional rest breaks, and other accommodations for standardized tests such as the SAT and GRE. Doctors can use reports to adjust their treatment plans, including medication management. Speech, occupational, and physical therapists can see what exactly their therapies have targeted and what remains a growth edge. Counselors can get additional insight on the child's psychological functioning. This report serves as a broad and yet in-depth examination of your child's functioning that is applicable on many levels.

Another sometimes underappreciated aspect of the evaluation is the benefit of a retest. Scores are perhaps most informative about functioning when they change over time. A single evaluation can provide estimates on what might have changed but without a second evaluation, it is impossible to firmly established what actually has changed. Retesting, particularly after some kind of intervention, can provide valuable insights on how your child has progressed and which areas still need to be addressed. Chapter 3 describes how neuropsychologists interpret test results within the report.

As might be expected, neuropsychologists write neuropsychological reports. However, sometimes parents will read reports that are "psychodiagnostic," or "educational," or even "psychoeducational." What exactly differentiates these reports? The truth is, there is no easy answer as there are not any strict regulations on what psychologists must call their reports. However, some general guidelines can be offered.

Neuropsychological Evaluation: These evaluations assess IQ, achievement, and several cognitive domains such as memory, attention, and executive functioning (see Chapter 5 for details on these terms). Academic achievement is also addressed. Most neuropsychologists also assess for emotional functioning. This report tends to be the most comprehensive, and is the most likely to address more difficult referral questions including ones in which a medical illness is involved. If your child has significant learning issues, notable neurological or medical history, multiple disorders, or there is a need to rule out one or more multiple diagnosis, then this evaluation would best suit your needs.

Psychoeducational/Educational Evaluation: These evaluations, which can be conducted by any qualified psychologist, usually just include IQ and achievement testing, with less emphasis on other cognitive domains and emotional functioning. The reports are often sufficient in addressing questions of learning disabilities and ADHD and suffice for requests for accommodations. Sometimes, psychoeducational reports are more comprehensive and resemble neuropsychological evaluations.

Psychodiagnostic Evaluation: This is the classical term used for assessments and does not require any cognitive testing. Psychodiagnostic evaluations are primarily concerned with personality and emotional functioning and will typically look for depression, anxiety, and other underlying psychological conditions. Sometimes, cognitive testing is included in this evaluation although usually it is minimal in nature. Therefore, this type of evaluation is most suitable when achievement and cognition are not a concern while emotional functioning is the question at hand. Please be aware that some clinicians will interchangeably use the terms "psychodiagnostic" and "psychoeducational" when referring to the same report.

Intellectual Assessment: Some programs and schools only admit children who surpass a cutoff score on an IQ test. IQ tests usually take 1.5-2.5 hours depending on the child's performance. If the sole purpose of an evaluation is to obtain this score for admittance to such a program, then any qualified psychologist is eligible to conduct this assessment. Due to the straightforward nature of the questions, the cost of such a service should be considerably lower than a full evaluation. However, IQ tests alone will tell you little about your child (other than whether he or she can enter a program). See Chapter 4 for more discussion on intelligence tests.

Ask your practitioner which type of evaluation is most suitable for your needs. Some professionals conduct all of these services (even at

varying costs) while others might refer to a colleague who would be a better match for your child.

The Where

At first, the setting for an assessment might seem less important than other factors, but it merits some consideration. Assessments can be conducted at hospitals and mental health clinics. Such settings have highly trained individuals, many who conduct research and teach, and are more likely to take insurance. On the other hand, there is often less access to practitioners and wait times for some centers can be lengthy. Hospitals might also be intimidating for children and are not always necessary, particularly when a school-related evaluation is requested.

Most private practitioners will have an office that is designed for assessments. Look for rooms that are soundproof and welcoming. Chairs and other furniture should be child-sized and child-friendly. Toys, books, and a friendly office staff will also ensure that your child is comfortable and will perform to his or her best during the examination.

Some parents raise the question of in-home assessments. There are different perspectives on this – on the positive side, such assessments usually guarantee that the child will be very comfortable. Comfort allows for a stronger measure of test results and a more successful evaluation. However, there are more random factors that can interfere with the evaluation. Pets, phone calls, and other family members might distract the child (see footnote 3). Houses are not always easily set up for testing. If you would like an in-home assessment, speak with your practitioner and see if it is an option. If it is, try to find a quiet room where your child won't be overly distracted. There should be comfortable chairs and a low, wide table where the tests can be easily administered.

Assessments at school have the convenience of minimizing time away from school. If the child likes his or her school, it sometimes can also be relaxing due to its familiarity. At the same time, one must be mindful that other children are around and some may notice your child engaging in a different activity. Children who are self-conscious might be reluctant to undergo testing where their friends might notice them. If the neuropsychologist has a good relationship with the school and you trust that this relationship will help your child, then it may be an option but speak with everyone involved (including your child) to ascertain whether this is a good option.

The When

There are two 'whens' to consider; when during the day, and when during your child's life. With regard to the day, keep in mind that each session usually runs between 2-8 hours. Clarify with the neuropsychologist the number of days and estimated length of each session. A full eight-hour session is generally not recommended unless your child is an older adolescent or adult with few attentional issues. When splitting up the evaluation, it's best to do the evaluation early in day so the child is as fresh as possible to focus on the tests. Sometimes, testing has to be done after school and/or in the evening. If so, a competent neuropsychologist would make note of this, along with any other external factors that might impact performance.

The age at which you bring your child for an assessment often depends on the referral question. Many of the tests are unreliable in very young children. For example, standard IQ and achievement tests are less likely to produce stable scores in children who are under six. Therefore, formal assessments of academic delays and learning disabilities might be a bit premature until a child has completed kindergarten, or even the first grade. Children who are between 2-4 years of age are often referred due to behavioral and communication concerns. Issues relating to social behavior, impulsivity, and hyperactivity might be raised. Trained practitioners can detect signs of an autistic spectrum disorder around this age with accuracy. Therefore, the question of an autistic spectrum disorder is an appropriate one to answer when evaluating a child of this age.

Other conditions, such as ADHD, developmental coordination disorders, and communication disorders, might be investigated, but at such a young age any diagnoses should generally be provisional in nature. There are a number of reasons that children might act out at this age and many factors must be considered before coming to one of these diagnoses. In addition, some children develop a bit slower than others and so may initially exhibit problematic behaviors in preschool that resolve as the child matures.

Elementary school is a time when learning issues often emerge. If a child does have an attentional issue, it will emerge more prominently the older the child becomes. Elementary schools typically start assigning more responsibilities, such as homework, around the second or third grade and this is when ADHD may particularly impact school achievement. A second "risk" period in elementary school occurs towards its end, as the child begins the transition towards middle school. Homework assignments often become more conceptual and self-initiated, and social pressures may further impact schoolwork as the child begins to navigate the challenges of adolescence.

Adolescence, of course, comes with its pressures and responsibilities. Children with milder attentional or learning issues might struggle more as midterms, final exams, and take-home projects become more frequent. Many of these undiagnosed youths with high intelligence and motivation can often navigate through elementary school on their own, but begin to buckle under the pressures of middle and high school. Adolescents have more responsibility structuring their time around a busy schedule of school, friendships, sports, and other extracurricular activities. This is a challenge for virtually all teenagers and may particularly impact those who have undiagnosed conditions. Even if a cognitive or learning diagnosis is not involved, adolescents still have to navigate the complex social and academic demands placed on them, and a comprehensive evaluation can provide insights on how a teenager best learns and what can be implemented to help him or her thrive.

Many parents (and their children) express interest in an evaluation for the college years. Such evaluations, whether they are conducted right before college or by the end of freshman year, can be instrumental in providing academic accommodations that will help address any learning issues. Finally, even the post-college young adult might benefit from an evaluation to provide a path towards occupational success, as well as identify underlying emotional or personality factors that might be contributing to current problems.

An evaluation can be informative at virtually any stage of a child's development. In my opinion, there are particularly crucial transitional years when issues might emerge. These include preschool, second/third grade, sixth grade, and tenth/eleventh grade. Generally speaking, these years usually coincide with major academic shifts at school, as well as developmental changes in children themselves. Such transitions are always a risk factor for new problems to emerge and for a previously undiagnosed issue to become more prominent.

Finally, parents sometimes wonder when in the school year an evaluation is most appropriate. It is sometimes premature to evaluate a child who just started a new grade (see "The Why" section below) as children often struggle initially and then settle into a routine. A good time to begin the process of an evaluation would be about 6–8 weeks into the school year if the problem still persists, at which point it is still early enough in the year to implement accommodations in the fall. If the evaluation is not conducted by then, it should be done at least prior to the next quarter/semester so that accommodations can be implemented by then. Late spring and summer are often good times as well, both in terms of your schedule and the school's schedule, so that preparations can be made for the following year. Please note that if you are seeking testing accommodations for your child, it's best to have a copy of the report in your hands a full quarter (i.e. three months) prior to the next exam. This provides all parties ample time to prepare and process paperwork, as well as make petitions should any complications arise.

The Why (Nots)

"The Why" is quite broad and much of this book addresses why you might have your child assessed. Therefore, it might be useful to discuss some of the "Why Nots," or circumstances when a neuropsychological evaluation is *not* necessarily the best route to take.

During transitional periods: Children typically prefer routine, and disruptions in routine can be frightening and upsetting. It is perfectly normal to see a change in your child during major transitions, such as a new school, a new home, or a new addition to the family. At the start of the semester, new teachers and new expectations might be an initial struggle for children. Most children will adapt within a month or so and it might be premature to seek an assessment prior to this month passing.

Reevaluating a child for accommodations when there is little change: This is a bit trickier, because neuropsychologists are certainly an appropriate referral to assess your child when you are seeking additional accommodations. I believe the key word here is "reevaluate," such that a learning disability or another diagnosis has already been established, and you already have a report in your hand. If your child is progressing reasonably well in school, and you simply wish to undergo a revaluation so that he or she may eligible for accommodations at a new high school or college, then a psychoeducational report (e.g. just IQ and achievement testing) would likely suffice. However, if additional complications that emerge, from either a learning, cognitive, or emotional level, then a full neuropsychological evaluation would be more appropriate.

There is minimal cognitive concern: Sometimes, the issue at hand is clearly emotional, with little concern for a cognitive change. For example, a middle schooler who is experiencing depression and some substance use might be academically underperforming, but if he did very well up until these recent events, then a full neurocognitive battery may not be warranted. This child certainly should see a mental health professional to help overcome obstacles, but unless there is a suspected cognitive issue contributing to the problem (which there very well might be in some circumstances), then it is uncertain what a neuropsychological evaluation would contribute above and beyond a standard intake during therapy. Do note that in younger children, cognitive disturbances are more difficult to outright observe as they sometimes manifest as behavioral problems, and so an evaluation may be more appropriate to rule out a diagnoses.

Within a year after an evaluation: Unless you are seeking a second opinion, reevaluations should be spaced apart. The exact timing for this varies depending on the nature of the issue, but in general you want to let at least a year pass to allow your child to further develop and benefit from tutoring. There are some exceptions, such as when a child is in a crisis mode or has suffered a severe neurological injury (see footnote 4), although usually shorter batteries that primarily focus on acute disturbances are then appropriate.

FOOTNOTE 1

The Houston Guidelines (discussed in the appendix) mandate the following requirements for a neuropsychologist to be board eligible. First, they must have a doctoral degree in psychology and have a license to practice as a psychologist. They then have to engage in a two-year postdoctoral program (or its equivalent over a longer period of time). Such programs can be at a formal training institute or a private practice. Fellows must demonstrate competency across eight knowledge areas that include aspects of neuroscience, psychology, and neurology. During their postdoctoral studies, at least 50% of their time must involve neuropsychological evaluation under the supervision of another neuropsychologist. All applicants must submit their credentials to the American Board of Clinical Neuropsychology (ABCN) who review it. Eligible applicants are invited to formally apply, which involves passing a written and oral examine and submitting de-identified reports for panel review.

FOOTNOTE 2

Parents might notice that relatively few private child neuropsychologists take insurance, in part because it can be difficult to obtain reimbursement, Insurance often pays only a small portion of what a neuropsychologist typically charges, and some companies will deny services that are not deemed to be medically necessary (as school-related evaluations can be perceived). At the same time, neuropsychologists who do take insurance often find the experience rewarding as they can serve additional families and the community, and often the reimbursement is enough to make a reasonable living. If a neuropsychologist does not take insurance, see if they are willing to provide you with a "superbill," which can be submitted to your insurance company as the services of an out-of-network provider. Depending on your policy, you may be reimbursed a portion of your cost, although this is not a guarantee. If you are trying to save money, speak to both your insurance company about out-of-network reimbursement, and to your neuropsychologist to see if you can find a situation that is satisfactory for all parties.

FOOTNOTE 3

I sometimes engage in in-home assessments, particularly when there might be a clinically indicated reason. One way to handle these situations is to take everything that happens during the assessment as a possible indicator of something (e.g. everything is "grist for the mill," so to speak). I remember evaluating one young boy in his parents' kitchen. Unfortunately, during a timed test of sustained attention and concentration, the family dog broke in and started barking at something outside. To my surprise, my patient was able to maintain his focus on this test and performed well above the average range - certainly a pertinent observation if there ever was one!

FOOTNOTE 4

Traumatic brain injury is a very frightening prospect for parents. Fortunately, most injuries are mild in nature and have few if any longstanding problems (see Chapter 13 for more detail). Sometimes, however, the injury is severe enough that there is a real possibility of permanent damage. Most children will make their most profound gains in the first few months, with progress slowing by the end of the first year after injury. Studies have shown that there is minimal recovery of lost functions by the end of the first year. Therefore, frequent and brief assessments between the first few weeks after injury up to the first year can objectively measure recovery patterns. Note that such assessments will almost always be done in a medical setting, with little need to include an outside private practitioner (unless you are seeking an evaluation well after recovery is completed).

CHAPTER 2

Myths, Facts, and Questions to Ask

There are a number of myths about the negative effects of an evaluation. This chapter will dispel some of the more common ones.

Myth 1: "This evaluation will put a label on my child."

Parents may fear that testing will show that their child is slow, or behind, or a "problem student" and that such results will have long lasting negative consequences. For example, such children might be denied admittance to school or college or be placed in the "bad group" at school. While understandable, such fears are usually unfounded. First of all, parents own the rights to their child's evaluation and therefore have control over who can read it. This should assuage any concerns that findings or possible diagnoses will be made public; if you don't want anyone else to know the results then that is your right as the legal guardian.

Furthermore, a child who has a real learning or cognitive issue will struggle if this issue is not identified – at best, they might just consistently be behind in school while at worst, they might be accused of being lazy or unmotivated, be ostracized by teachers and peers, and may lose self-esteem. These are the real negative consequences that all too often occur when the real problem is not identified. Finally, testing doesn't just reveal weaknesses – a child's personal strengths also shine through in the evaluation. By identifying these strengths, they can be celebrated with the child and used to help compensate for any actual weaknesses that may exist.

Myth 2: "The school wants an evaluation to find a reason to tell us that our child isn't a fit for them."

It is unlikely for an evaluation to be a determinant in making such a difficult decision, because evaluations are generally recommended when teachers have identified an issue with your child and want more information on how to best help him or her thrive in class. As such, evaluations are preventative– by learning your child's strengths and weaknesses, this helps teachers, parents, and ultimately the child him/herself work better at the school.

Myth 3: "My child's self-esteem will be hurt by the evaluation."

As mentioned, a child's strengths as well as personal weaknesses are identified. Many neuropsychologists are willing to provide age-appropriate feedback directly to your child and highlight findings. Speaking personally, my most profound feedbacks were directly to the child, who learned a few new things about him or herself and took the positive news to heart with longstanding improvements.

Myth 4: "My child will inevitably be diagnosed with ADHD if s/he undergoes an evaluation."

It is true that ADHD can be overdiagnosed. However, just because there may be an overabundance of diagnoses does not invalidate the condition itself. Suspicion of ADHD is certainly a common reason why children are referred for an evaluation, but for most psychologists it is but one of several possible explanations. Adjusting to life changes, mood and emotional factors, and learning disorders are other frequent explanations for what may initially seem like an attentional diagnosis. Even if ADHD is the ultimate explanation for what is going on, it is much better to have the right answer rather than hope that it is simply a phase that will eventually go away on its own.

Myth 5: "The evaluation might diagnose my child but what's the point? A diagnosis won't do anything for my child."

A diagnosis is only the first step towards building an intervention plan, but it is an important one. It is true that a diagnoses by itself without further action will do little good. On the flip side, a diagnoses alone is not a 'magic bullet'. It is a conduit towards having a conversation with the parents, teachers, learning specialists and the child themselves.

Questions to Ask

Here are some sample questions you may want to ask your neuropsychologist. This is not exhaustive and not all questions will pertain to your situation, but these can serve as a starting point.

1 Did you complete a neuropsychology fellowship?

2 Are you board certified in neuropsychology? If not, are you board eligible?

3 How many years have you been in practice?

4 What kind of populations do you work with?

5 What settings have you worked at? Hospitals? Private practices? Schools?

6   Tell me a bit about your assessment process:

  a How long do your assessments take?

  b How many visits can we anticipate, and how long should each visit be?

  c Do you conduct school observations?

  d What is your turnaround time for reports?

  e Will you be willing to speak to my child's teachers, pediatricians, etc?

  f Who is involved during the feedback session?

  g Are you available for follow-up after the assessment is completed?

7   How much do you charge for your services?

  a Do you take insurance?

  b Do you offer a different rate for different services (e.g. a shorter battery for a reevaluation or an IQ test)?

  c Do you charge a flat rate for all services?

8   Do you ever do in-home assessments? Would you do an assessment at my child's school?

9   Is this a good time for my child's assessment? Should we wait or should we schedule something as soon as possible?

10   Do you think that a full neuropsychological evaluation will help figure out what is going on?

CHAPTER 3

The How

An evaluation is a complex process. This chapter will explain the steps involved on both sides. Please note this is a fictional account that merges several experiences I've had as a trainee and as a private practitioner. It is by no means a template of an evaluation, but rather serves as an example of one way it might proceed.

Rachel's son, Jimmy, has had a difficult start to the second grade. His math teacher said that he is not grasping subtraction with two digit numbers and recommends tutoring. Jimmy is expressing anxiety about leaving mom at morning drop-off, something that hasn't happened since early first grade. Complicating matters is Jimmy's dad, who has missed three of the last four weekends he was supposed to take custody of his son. Rachel herself is stressed about her job and about her older son, who has his own troubles.

There are many reasons to seek an evaluation. Whatever they are, they usually come with anxiety and concern from parents and the child. *Something* is not right, and whether it is something that has been going on for a long time or just recently, you want some answers. Maybe possible answers themselves are worrying - a diagnosis, or a medical condition, or maybe something that you could have done differently. But you love your child, and you hope that this evaluation will shed some light on what is going on and provide guidance on the next steps to take.

> By October, Jimmy has started throwing tantrums before going to school. In addition, both his math and reading teachers have gently told Rachel that he seems to struggle keeping up with the other students. Rachel agrees to a parent-teacher conference, where Jimmy's reading teacher described a recent time when Jimmy was in a reading group and was the last one to finish his worksheet. He saw that he was the last one and so started crying in class. Rachel herself knows that Jimmy is saying that he is "stupid" and he hates school during his tantrums. She tells the school psychologist this, who agrees that Jimmy seems to be developing a poor self-image of his abilities. She recommends that Jimmy undergo a neuropsychological evaluation to see if there are any explanations for his recent struggles.

When you make the decision to see a specialist, you might wonder how to convey what an evaluation is to your child. There is no single answer, as it depends on the age of your child and his or her ability to understand what an evaluation is. For very young children, it sometimes helps to tell them that they are seeing a teacher or a learning expert. You can phrase it in a way that relates to something the child knows about (i.e. "Remember how you sometimes struggle with multiplication? Dr. Smith can help you with that!"). You can reassure them that this is not a typical "doctor's visit" with no shots or pills, and that they will be playing lots of games to see how they best learn.

> Rachel speaks with three neuropsychologists and identifies one who seems the best fit for Jimmy. Dr. Yu has been in practice for ten

years and she has a good relationship with Jimmy's school. During the initial conversation, Dr. Yu said that Jimmy should have a good night's rest and a full breakfast prior to the first day. Rachel tells Jimmy that Dr. Yu is a learning doctor who can help him do better in school. Jimmy was nervous and unfortunately didn't sleep well the night before, but he was okay during the drive to the office. Right before entering the office, Jimmy suddenly froze and clutched his mom's arm. She half walked, half dragged Jimmy into the waiting room. There were lots of toys in the waiting room but Jimmy only had eyes for his mom. He silently shook his head at her.

Many factors will affect test performance (see footnote 1). Open communication will help the doctor integrate these into the evaluation. At the same time, it is completely normal for your child to be anxious right before the evaluation and this typically will not invalidate the results.

Rachel is impressed by Dr. Yu's warm demeanor. Dr. Yu gets down on one knee and thanks Jimmy for agreeing to come. He seems less anxious and his grip on mom loosens a bit. Dr. Yu, who introduces herself as Stacy, tells Jimmy that they will be playing lots of games today and he might win some prizes. She learns that Jimmy likes Spiderman and promises he might win a Spiderman toy or two if he works real hard today. She then takes Rachel and Jimmy into her office. She provides Rachel with two rating forms, one that she asks Rachel to deliver to one of Jimmy's teachers. They outline the day, which will start with an interview with Rachel, and about two hours of testing with Jimmy.

Practitioners have their own styles. Some have a full office staff while others work on their own. Some introduce themselves as "doctor" while others (like the one in this vignette) are fine with a first-name basis. Some will use games and prizes as a way to motivate the children to make a good effort. Sometimes, the neuropsychologist does not conduct all the testing themselves but instead have a specially trained assistant (i.e. psychometrician) or trainee help out (see footnote 2). Regardless, all neuropsychologists will oversee the testing and interpretation of scores and will personally conduct the interviews and the feedback.

Rachel and Stacy start their interview while Jimmy goes back to the waiting room under the watchful eye of the receptionist. Rachel finds herself pouring all of her own recent frustrations out – her ex-husband's absence in their lives, her older son's struggles with alcohol, her job stressors. She knows that the focus is on Jimmy but finds herself relating Jimmy's issues with those within the family. During this process, she suddenly sees the big picture of how many of Jimmy's issues are reflective of the family conflict, and she is quick to bring this to Stacy's attention. Stacy mostly lets Rachel speak but offers empathy and at one point, pauses the interview to get Rachel some water. She asks questions about Jimmy's development, including his birth and early milestones. She asks about Jimmy's social history (friends, siblings) and school history. The entire interview takes about 75 minutes. Rachel also provides consent for Stacy to contact Jimmy's teachers and pediatrician.

There are many things to look for during an evaluation. Test scores, while informative, only capture a small portion of the assessment. Along with the actual scores, we factor in behavioral observations during testing. These observations look at a number of things, such as eye contact, rate/tone/volume of speech, fine and gross motor skills, general expressive and receptive abilities, mood/affect, anxiety, and thought processes just to name a few. Earlier I mentioned that our tests really just measure behavior (with the design of capturing cognitive expressions of behavior). Good observations are therefore instrumental to come to an accurate conclusion.

Stacy and Jimmy begin the evaluation. First, Stacy asks Jimmy a few basic questions, like his age, his family, his school, and his hobbies. Jimmy is visibly nervous and only provides one-word answers at first. He also keeps looking at the door and at one point asks where his mommy is. He smiles when Stacy brings out some toys and they talk a bit about the latest superhero movie. Stacy watches Jimmy slowly relax and become more animated and they discussed the merits of Captain America and the X-Men. Stacy notes that Jimmy really likes superheroes and identifies with some more than others — for example, he sees a bit of Captain America in him. When asked why, he says that Captain America was really weak before but became strong and now uses his strength to do good. Jimmy agreed this is what he tries to do at school. Stacy also notes that Jimmy's thought processes are pretty organized and he can follow a conversation pretty well. She tries switching topics to his family. She gently asks about his father and Jimmy lights up and talks about his dad's work and how he and his dad love miniature golf. When talking about his mother, Jimmy also looks happy but says he sometimes gets mad at her because she keeps him from seeing his father.

Family dynamics inevitably emerge during an evaluation. Sometimes, these dynamics can come to a surprise to parents and sometimes, they come as unpleasant surprises. Neuropsychologists are ethically bound to report their findings in the report to the best of their knowledge and ability. This is different from legal mandates towards break confidentiality (see footnote 3) but essentially holds us practitioners responsible for reporting accurate findings and addressing all aspects that might help in answering the referral question.

That said, information can be sensitive and not all of it may be necessary to share with third parties. Tailored reports (which explicitly note they are tailored) can omit more personal factors if the intent of sharing a report is to help with accommodations, such as the case at schools. Speak with your practitioner if and when the issue arises to see if this can be an option – most neuropsychologists are amenable to write an abridged version of the report.

After forty-five minutes, Stacy has a number of observations about Jimmy. She notes that he started out anxious but was quick to warm up. He is a sweet child with a friendly disposition. No social issues were observed in this specific environment. His fine and gross motor skills were developmentally appropriate. He clearly is experiencing some turmoil related to his parents' separation and his brother's behavior. School is indeed becoming an overwhelming factor in his life and Jimmy doesn't feel like he is capable and so is starting to dislike going to school. Without giving a single test, Stacy has the impression that Jimmy is likely a bright boy who does struggle in some academic areas – these struggles, along with stress at home, has been quite difficult. Stacy does not yet know the nature or extent of these problems. Some of that will come to light during testing.

There are hundreds of tests available, although most practitioners use a similar battery and likely draw from a pool of about 40–50 tests. Most are pencil and paper or on a desktop or other computer device. Tests are generally designed to capture one or more aspects of cognition, including IQ, attention, processing speed, visual/verbal memory, working memory, visual-spatial abilities, expressive and receptive language, executive functions, fine motor abilities, social cognition, and emotional/personality.

Stacy starts with a picture completion test, a test that requires kids to find a missing detail in a scene. Jimmy enjoys the test and wins a sticker at the end, which he can later trade in for a prize. His mood relaxes and so Stacy moves on to the more challenging test of assembling blocks to match a design. She observes that Jimmy takes his time on this test but has trouble rotating the blocks efficiently, ultimately giving up when the test becomes more difficult. They proceed with many other tests, some of which challenge Jimmy's verbal abilities, others which look into his attention and speed of processing. Throughout the tests, Jimmy has a pattern of giving up when he feels uncertain about something, with a preference to not respond rather than guess. She notes that Jimmy seems a bit better with verbal information and struggles with abstract, visual tests. She also observes that despite his relatively high intellect, he's a bit slower at processing information compared to other boys his age.

Some common learning styles that testing will identify will include a preference for verbal versus visual information, discrepancies between working memory and processing speed, fine motor inter-ferences, language processing issues, and strengths/weaknesses in executive functioning. You might learn that your child jumps to conclusions but can get a problem right if given a second chance – or that your child thinks very fast but has trouble encoding information into memory as a result. Some children are more comfortable with concrete information while others like to think "outside the box" and perform very well on the more abstract tests. Other children might be quite gifted in ways that are hidden by their high level of energy and lack of focus.

The first day of testing ends without issue. Jimmy proudly shows his new Spiderman wristwatch to his mom. When asked, he says that Dr. Stacy is "really nice" and his new friend and he can't wait for the second assessment, scheduled three days from now. Rachel is relieved that Jimmy is enjoying the process but is also growing anxious about what the results might say about her son. On the second day of testing, Jimmy runs up to Stacy and gives her a big hug. The two adults exchange pleasantries and then Stacy takes Jimmy back for more testing. He wins more prizes, and the testing now is more focused on academics. Stacy notes that Jimmy can read single words without difficulty, but he struggles pronouncing phonemes of nonsense words.

He also switches letters while writing and spelling, and has some comprehension struggles. This translates to some issues misreading arithmetic signs. Notably, Jimmy is at a loss with grade-appropriate word problems and resumes his pattern of giving up. To compensate for this, Stacy ends the day with some more fun tests. They break for the day.

Achievement tests look at single-word reading, general reading comprehension, oral reading skills, basic math skills, problem-solving, spelling, and expressive writing among other abilities. The term "achievement" refers to abilities that children generally learn at school, versus "aptitude" which represents general cognitive potential. Generally, aptitude tests explain performance on achievement tests, which directly map onto school performance. Like all tests, achievement scores are compared to a general cohort of children who are of a similar age and grade-level as the assessed child.

Between the second and third evaluation, Stacy follows up with Jimmy's teachers. She conducts two interviews and learns that Jimmy's mood really depends on his father – Mondays are a particularly hard time for Jimmy when his father cancels on him. They discuss scheduling a school visit, although this is ultimately not arranged as the teachers report that Jimmy is well behaved in class and gets along well with the other children. Stacy speaks briefly with the pediatrician, who confirms that Jimmy has always been a physically healthy baby and young boy. The third evaluation is brief, only two hours, and Stacy wraps up a few of the achievement tests that were not completed. She closes with some projective tests in which Jimmy is asked to interpret some images. When shown a card of a mother holding a baby, Jimmy says that the "mom and baby are holding each other real tight, because the mom loves him and the baby is feeling scared." When seeing a picture of a man teaching a young girl to ride her bike, he says "that man is helping the girl with a bike." When further prompted about their relationship, Jimmy hesitated and said "it could be her dad, or maybe a stranger."

Projective testing is one way to understand what a child might be going through. Self report forms and a thorough interview may suffice for older children. Regardless, the input from parents, teachers, and other professionals is invaluable in accurately assessing a child's emotional health. Some practitioners also engage in play therapy, such as sandbox play (see footnote 4) for younger and nonverbal children.

The evaluation is complete. Stacy spends the next three weeks reading through her notes and interpreting the test data. As anticipated, Jimmy's verbal IQ is quite high, at the 82nd percentile (higher than 81 out of every 100 children who are Jimmy's age). His fluid reasoning is also fine, at the 55th percentile. Jimmy's processing speed, or speed which he completes tests, varies from the 10th percentile to the 63rd percentile. This variability suggests that he doesn't have a globally slow work style but rather, his speed fluctuates depending on his state and the nature of the test. Working memory, or the ability to hold and manipulate information, is low at the 12th percentile. On academics, Jimmy's single-word reading and comprehension of short sentences were fine, but he struggled reading unfamiliar words and longer passages. His spelling was behind, at a 1st grade level, and the quality of his written output was low. On the positive side, his memory was strong, and he was not impulsive on any executive tests. Based on this data, Stacy concludes that Jimmy has a reading disability characterized by difficulties processing phonemes. The source of this difficulty appears to stem from lower than expected performance on auditory working memory, rather than processing speed. Jimmy's school anxiety translates towards test anxiety, which lowers his scores across several subjects, but in truth his mathematical abilities are not a primary concern. In fact, his difficulties with word problems stem from *reading, not from math. Not surprisingly, Jimmy is also experiencing some depression that is related to the upheaval of his parents' divorce and his father's absence. Along with a reading disorder, he meets criteria for an adjustment disorder with depressed mood.*

Diagnoses are important for insurance reimbursements, certain accommodations (particularly those granted at the state or federal level), and to better clarify the underlying problem in terms that doctors, teachers, and other professionals can understand. At the same time, the diagnoses themselves sometimes are the least import-ant aspect of the report for the parents, who simply want to know how to help their child. Giving the cluster of presented symptoms a name is a step in the right direction, but many different children with unique presentations might fall under the same diagnosis. The neuropsychological evaluation is designed to go further than just diagnosing, by providing a roadmap on how to best help your child with his or her issues.

Jimmy and Rachel come in for feedback. As discussed prior on the phone, Jimmy will stay for the first few minutes for some basic feedback. Rachel watches with some amusement as Jimmy and Stacy engage in their superhero rapport. Stacy then tells Jimmy that he is actually quite smart and that he did very well on several of the tests. She adds that his brain can think fast and sometimes, parts of it thinks too fast for other parts to catch up. This might explain why reading is sometimes tricky, because his brain is already reading ahead while his mind is trying to catch up. Stacy uses the analogy of boys running in a race – Jimmy's brain is the sprinter, chugging along real fast while the "mind" (here presented as Jimmy's conscious awareness) is trying to play catch up. Stacy adds that Jimmy should try to slow down with reading so his mind can catch up to the raw physical power of his brain. Jimmy is delighted to learn that he has a "fast" brain.

Often, presenting feedback directly to the child can have the most powerful effect. After all, your child is the one going through all the tests, and so any results are most directly applicable to him or her! There is no age limit in conveying feedback, so long as it is done conscientiously and at an age-appropriate level. Some neuropsychologists even bring in plastic brains or drawings of brains for a physical demonstration of how exactly how the brain works. Most importantly, a well-conveyed message to kids can have longstanding effects, particularly when self-esteem is a concern. Just imagine you as a child, with a grown doctor highlighting your strengths and talents. Who wouldn't be impressed with themselves?

Feedback continues with just the adults. Stacy provides more frank information to Rachel. She explains the nature of Jimmy's reading disorder, which fits a pattern similar to classic dyslexia (see footnote 5). She explains that Jimmy can think fast, but his auditory working memory is lower than what might be expected. Several recommendations are provided. First, school accommodations are recommended: Jimmy should have more time on reading assignments, and he should be graded for content over spelling. The school's reading specialist can provide Jimmy with outside tutoring. Strategies for improving working memory, such as the use of "chunking" and other techniques are reviewed. Furthermore, Stacy brings up Jimmy's recent depression. Rachel admits that recently, he has begun to complain of stomachaches and as of last week, asked to go home early from school because of one. She agreed that Jimmy is going through a hard time with all the family conflict. Stacy offers to put Rachel in contact with a local child therapist who she believes would be a great match for Rachel's son. Finally, Rachel is assured that her son is quite bright, with a wonderful disposition. He has some reading struggles and school anxiety, which in part stems from stress at home, but with collaboration from Rachel, Stacy, Jimmy's teachers, and the school learning specialist, every effort will be made to ensure that Jimmy will have a smoother experience during second grade.

Feedback only works when there is follow through on all ends. Do not hesitate to reach out to the neuropsychologist after feedback to clarify any remaining questions, or follow up on outside referrals and services. Here is where the neuropsychologist can really serve within the community – by having close ties with other psychologists, educators, and schools, he or she can be a lifelong advocate.

Life goes on after the evaluation. Rachel has a talk with Jimmy's father who seems to take some of the feedback to heart. He's more consistent now, although he still skips some visits and Jimmy's mood still takes a hit. Fortunately, Jimmy has hit it off with his new therapist, who he sees once a week. His attitude towards school is a bit better. His teachers let him take on more responsibility with group projects – his social skills and his verbal intelligence make him suited as a leader, which builds his confidence. His in-class assignments are praised for their content with less focus on spelling. However, spelling is directly addressed with the school learning specialist, who meets with Jimmy twice a week. His reading is slowly improving and his math (which was never behind to begin with after all) is accelerating. There are still bad days and occasional tantrums, but they are less now. Rachel also feels she has a grip on Jimmy's strengths and weaknesses, and is hopeful for a smooth transition to the spring semester.

As I said at the outset of this chapter, every evaluation is different and presents with unique circumstances. This fictional example had a positive outlook in part because many people, including Jimmy's mother and the teachers, were onboard in helping Jimmy out and that Jimmy is in an enriched environment where specialists and therapists are readily available. Even his absent father changed his behavior, which isn't always the case. In some situations, the other divorced parent might want to be more involved with the evaluation, which often requires additional considerations.

This chapter provided a step-by-step walkthrough of a sample evaluation. You have read several terms here, such as "intelligence," "achievement," and "executive functioning." These next two chapters will tackle exactly what is meant by these terms.

FOOTNOTE 1

Test anxiety, depression, lack of sleep, too much sleep. These are just some of the things that can affect scores. Quite a bit rides on a very constrained period of time – in just a few hours, data that can impact your child's future will be collected and tabulated. Perhaps your child is allergic to dogs, and another psychologist renting the office brought in a therapy dog the other day. Maybe there are other children playing outside. Maybe the examiner reminds the child of a favorite (or least favorite) aunt. Perhaps it just isn't your child's day, and he decides he will goof off and fail tests for fun. Regardless of the issue, much of the art in neuropsychology comes from understanding that test performance is variable and that scores are not absolute. Any accurate conclusion must be derived from patterns, not individual scores, and these patterns must be considered in the bigger picture of the nature and circumstances of the evaluation.

FOOTNOTE 2

Psychometrician is an official term for a trained professional in test administration. Some psychometricians work in research settings while others work in hospitals or in private practice. There are steps that need to be taken for certification and psychometricians are recognized in most states as a valid assessor for neuropsychological evaluations. Other neuropsychologists are involved in training programs (usually called practicums) in which trainees in psychology can practice assessment under supervision. These methods are sound and, under a competent supervisor, will yield effective data for assessment. Some psychometricians and trainees are trained to write down pertinent behavioral observations. Sometimes, the neuropsychologist will conduct a few of the initial tests before passing the rest to the employee. If you are uncertain about having someone other than the neuropsychologist conduct the evaluation, do not hesitate to ask questions about the process.

FOOTNOTE 3

All psychologists are mandated to break doctor-patient confidentiality in a few circumscribed situations. Although details vary somewhat state-by-state, exceptions to confidentiality include cases where the psychologist has a reasonable suspicion that the client may harm him or herself, harm another, identifiable victim, or when there is suspicion of either child or elder abuse.

FOOTNOTE 4

Sandplay is a form of play therapy that is less verbal than talk therapy. Children (and adults) are provided a sandbox in which they can express their feelings and thoughts using sand, water, and toys. This method is thought to represent an individual's internal world in a safe space. This is particularly helpful for individuals who are nonverbal, as with young children or those with pervasive developmental disorders.

FOOTNOTE 5

Dyslexia has an odd relationship with psychologists, as it is not an officially recognized learning disability in the DSM-5 diagnostic manual. While it is certainly a form of reading disability (which is a recognized diagnosis), not all reading disabilities are the same as dyslexia. This is because dyslexia focuses on phonics (i.e. how letters form into sounds and words). Visual processing issues are often a factor and individuals with dyslexia sometimes struggle in other subjects, such as arithmetic. Contrast this with a child who can read individual words and spell without difficulty, but has trouble processing longer passages – while this may also be a reading disability, this is not a classic presentation of "dyslexia." Do note that the term "dyslexia" is sometimes used interchangeably with a reading disorder, and so the two terms may mean the same thing, or not, depending on who is using these terms.

CHAPTER 4

IQ and Achievement

What is an IQ score? What does it measure and what does it predict? How is IQ different from achievement? This chapter addresses these questions.

The intelligence quotient, or "IQ" score, has a long history in assessment. The term IQ emerged early in our field and perhaps is one of the most captivating scores in a report. I've seen many clients skip through pages of text and tables only to rest their eyes on a single row: The Full Scale IQ score. Everyone wants a high IQ and no one wants a low IQ. There is a fear, particularly with parents and older adolescents, that whatever the Full Scale IQ is, it just isn't "good enough." It is understandable why this fear exists. The concept of an IQ score has permeated our culture and society. IQ scores are cutoffs for admittance to gifted programs. The Full Scale IQ is a factor in diagnosing an intellectual disability. We all see IQ tests offered on the Internet and you might have even taken a few for fun. It is certainly the most recognizable score in the sea of data presented within a report.

Jeff and Mary just received the results of their son Will's neuropsychological evaluation. The neuropsychologist is pleased to report that Will is bright with little evidence of an attentional or learning disorder. His recent school underachievement might be related to some social factors but from a testing perspective, he doesn't have any real hindrances to success. As he flips through the report, Jeff notes with some alarm that his son received a full scale IQ of 105, which the table also says puts him at the 63rd percentile of all 11-year old boys. His heart sinks as the doctor's voice fades to a buzz. Only 63rd? Jeff thinks back to his childhood, and how hard he had to work to finish college. He read recently that IQ is hereditary. Is this my fault? It certainly isn't from my wife's side – they are all doctors and lawyers! Jeff feels a panic in his throat as he imagines Will forever struggling in school, competing against all the 95th and 99th percentile kids and ultimately failing out of college. As he swallows the panic down, he maintains a stoic composure and glances at the doctor. It seems like they are wrapping up, but he still has so many questions to ask.

The full scale IQ score can be daunting, but it really should not be so. It is true that on a group level, these scores show some modest correlations with academic and occupational success. However, *much* of this is because children who score in the 60s and 70s on an IQ test (hence less than the 2nd percentile) will almost certainly face additional challenges in life. It is also true that some children with scores between 80-90 may struggle more at school – but some may not. There are many, many reasons why low scores might be obtained: culture, environment, and test familiarity all play a role (see footnote 1). In addition, IQ scores certainly do not capture all aspects of intelligence (see footnote 2). A lower score does not speak to an individual child's resilience, or creativity, or social skills. It does not speak to your child's drive to succeed.

The truth of the matter is that once you approach the average range of scores (i.e. 25th – 75th percentile), most children have the capacity to thrive well in society. Jeff, from the first vignette, really has little cause for concern. As the neuropsychologist mentioned, there wasn't evidence of any sort of learning disability, which is the important piece of the message. However, Jeff zeroed in on the "average" IQ score with rising panic. While the term "average" may not be very exciting in today's competitive society, it really just means "normal," such that you don't have to worry about any intellectual deficit hindering your child's future. Children with average, or what we call normal intelligence scores go on to succeed in college. Some obtain advanced degrees. Many are very successful in life. As always, IQ scores do not speak for your child's emotional health or future well-being. Therefore, I would treat a normal IQ as the equivalent of a routine checkup at the doctor. Normal blood pressure, cholesterol, and glucose levels are all desirable. Why not a normal IQ?

Jill is stunned to learn that her "lazy," underachieving daughter is actually quite gifted. She doesn't doubt the test scores, they are right in front of her. A 132 IQ? What does that even mean? It certainly doesn't reflect Beth's grades, which hovered around a B-/C+ all through middle school. She glances at her daughter as the doctor goes over the report, trying to read her implacable face. She hears talk about gifted programs, and fitting in better with like-minded peers. Jill wonders where this superior intelligence came from. She also wonders how it actually might be leveraged into something productive. As Beth waits in the waiting room, she asks the neuropsychologist about her daughter's underachievement. The doctor pauses and gently suggests that some of it is due to some underlying depression. Jill has long suspected this and is not surprised. What does surprise her is learning that her daughter is so used to learning things easily that she has become reluctant to challenge herself in school as the material becomes more difficult. "Is she too smart for her own good?" she wonders to herself.

What about the other end of the spectrum? Are high IQs universally good and meant to be coveted and (God forbid) paraded around like a badge? The literature does show that children with higher IQ scores are more likely to go on to higher education. Most MDs and PhDs have at least an above average IQ – scores around 120 are a good estimate of most professionals although to reiterate, many individuals with average IQs also succeed in these professions. There's also a bit of a prophetic quality with IQ scores – despite what we might think, IQ scores are not immutable biological traits that are present at birth and will never change. Scores can and will change, and factors such as the amount and quality education have great influence on IQ scores. So a question worth asking is, what came first, the PhD or the IQ score?

Education aside, there are a small sample of children who are, for one reason or another, preternaturally adept at these types of tests. Maybe they have excellent processing speed and working memory, so they think very quickly and can hold information in their heads for long periods of time. Maybe they were raised in a household that emphasized vocabulary and puzzles. Maybe they just *are.* Scores over 130 (i.e. better than 98 out of 100 same-age peers) are considered gifted, while those over 140 (i.e. better than 996 out of 1000 same-age peers) might fall into what we term "genius."

Having a high IQ comes with its own challenges. Children often find that learning comes easy to them, particularly in the earlier stages of school when academic rigor is less emphasized. They then might become more challenged in high school and college, where factors for success include motivation, responsibility, and consistency, and where a high IQ by itself is not enough. Many gifted children are aware early on that they are different from others. This can have social and emotional implications. Some children do adopt a "lazy" attitude – if it doesn't come to them easily, it's not worth doing at all. It may be related to self-esteem; performance is relative, and a child who is used to A's might balk at his first A- or B+. Sometimes, a high IQ comes at a cost of other abilities. We've all heard of the child who can discuss mathematics and philosophy with any adult at her parents' party and yet has no real friends of her own (see footnote 3). Whatever the situation, just as a lower IQ score doesn't confer failure, a high IQ score doesn't guarantee success.

So how should we interpret IQ scores? In the first two fictional vignettes the neuropsychologists failed to address the parents' unspoken concerns. Let's look at another example.

> *Bob and Mindy are surprised to learn that their son's full scale IQ is a 97 — this seems uncharacteristically low for their high-achieving child. However, Dr. Thakkar is quick to deemphasize this score. He explains that the FSIQ score is a composite of several other indexes, which in turn are composites of individual subtests. He highlights that their son's verbal intelligence is actually 118 (88th percentile), which is much more commensurate with how they perceive their child. However, his processing speed (i.e. speed on simple, timed tests) is low, at 79 (8th percentile), which may reflect both a cautious response style and a generally slow cognitive tempo. Dr. Thakkar goes on to explain that this style suggests that their child is very bright, especially in the verbal domain, but because his speed of thinking is slower than expected, the mental "gears" of his mind grind "fine and slow." In addition, other IQ indexes like perceptual reasoning and working memory are well within expectations. Therefore, their son has an edge in verbal comprehension and a relative weakness in processing speed, which fortunately does not compromise other aspects of his intellect.*

In the above vignette, Dr. Thakkar provides some background on this particular IQ test, which measures four domains of "intelligence" which in turn aggregate into a single score. As evident here, individual indexes vary quite widely and a single IQ score does not adequately capture how this particular child processes information. Even more importantly, it must be reemphasized that IQ tests are limited in the range of abilities they capture — the abilities they typically measure are ones that are important at school and some professions but they are by no means exhaustive. It is therefore important to understand the benefits and limitations of the intellectual assessment.

The achievement component of the assessment measures scholastic proficiency, in contrast to the "aptitude" tests of cognitive abilities that IQ tests purport to measure (see footnote 4). Achievement tests follow the standard curriculum of education at a national level. For example, children in second grade are expected to have certain proficiencies in reading, writing, and mathematics that extend beyond first grade but do not yet meet third grade expectations. Achievement tests often provide "grade equivalency" scores alongside standard scores (mean = 100, standard deviation = 15; see footnote 5) and percentiles, which can inform the estimated grade level your child is performing at in a given task. However, "grade level" refers to national standards, which may not apply to your child's school, particularly if it is an independent school that follows its own curriculum. This is one reason why it may be prudent to work with a professional who understands your school. Just because your child is testing at grade level does not mean he or she is thriving in the classroom.

Mikey's achievement scores reveal that he is testing above grade level in spelling and at grade level in written expression. His parents are somewhat (and happily) surprised because his teachers have been noting that Mikey's writing is somewhat sparse in content. He also tests at grade level in math. The neuropsychologist who saw him understands that at this particular school, children are encouraged to write more than expected at a public school and so she integrates this in making her recommendations. Here, his "average" writing score hides a possible delay in more advanced writing skills that might not be so apparent in a different school. In contrast, his "average" mathematical abilities are more consistent with the expectations of his school and so are less of an issue at this time.

Historically, learning disabilities were diagnosed when there was a sufficient discrepancy between IQ and achievement scores. This method has been discarded due to a number of problematic issues that emerged (see footnote 6). Learning disabilities are perhaps best diagnosed based on the integration of test scores, observations, teacher and parent reports, and context. Context is everything, because what might be adaptive and functional in one setting would not be so in another. This goes hand in hand with the social model of learning disabilities, such that there are cultural and environmental factors that will determine whether a child's learning struggles are truly "dysfunctional" (see footnote 7).

> *Adriano and Maria were delighted when their daughter Gabriela was accepted into the prestigious Westblue elementary program. They had just moved to California from Brazil on a work visa and all they heard about after moving in to their neighborhood was how desirable this particularly school was. Of course, Gabriela was always a stellar student in São Paulo and so it was little surprise that she would get into the top school in their new city. What did surprise them was the intense rigor of this new school – children were required to sit for lengthy hour-long lessons, back to back, with only a few breaks in between. Furthermore, the curriculum emphasized more memorization than what was expected at Gabriela's old school. It was only a matter of weeks before her parents were called in for a parent-teacher conference.*

It is perfectly understandable that sometimes, children thrive in one school and suddenly struggle in another. This can nonetheless be a frustrating and anxious experience for parents and the child. In Gabriela's case, her (perceived) struggles might be related to an actual learning disability that was previously undetected, adjustments due to a new country/house/school, differences in school cultures, language issues, or a mix of any of the above. Rest assured that in nearly all cases, there can be a solution that satisfies all parties involved.

Chapter 8 further discusses the multidisciplinary angle of assessment, where I highlight the mediating role that neuropsychologists can sometimes serve in these types of conversations.

> *For Ally, the results of the evaluation confirmed that she was reading two grade-levels behind her grade-matched peers. The evaluation uncovered primary weaknesses in phonological processing, single word oral reading accuracy, and slowed silent reading speed. Despite these reading decoding weaknesses, Ally was very smart and still able to understand much of what she read even when she struggled to pronounce the individual words. She was diagnosed with a specific learning disability in reading, and the report was shared with the school. The school responded by setting up an individualized education plan (IEP) that allowed Ally extra time on reading tests and a modified curriculum that emphasized problem-solving skills over heavy reading (e.g. in math class, Ally can have word problems read to her rather than reading them herself). Her teacher agreed to have her take the lead on math and art projects, which were her strengths, while lessening her requirement to read aloud in front of other children, which was known to affect her self-esteem. In addition, the school's reading specialist began meeting with Ally twice a month to bolster her phonological skills.*

Ultimately, the results of the evaluation can have a tremendous impact on your child's school experience. When parents, teachers, and professionals are all in sync with each other, great strides can be made in ensuring that children's scholastic, social, and emotional needs are all met in the best possible way.

In my opinion, interpreting academic achievement scores are a bit different from interpreting IQ scores. I always emphasize that IQ scores that are "average" are fine, for reasons described above. However, achievement scores generalize more directly to performance within the classroom and as a result, "average" or even "above average" achievement scores must be considered in the context of the child's actual functioning. It would be important to learn that Billy is "above average" in calculation when he is flunking his math tests. The knowledge that Billy has more advanced math skills than he demonstrates on his math tests is important to know. There must be some other explanation for his underachievement, such as attentional difficulties causing him to make careless errors, or purposefully failing to get more attention from his parents and teachers. It is also best to envision percentiles and grade-equivalency scores as your child's relative performance in the *national* level, which is just one of many indicators of proficiency at the *local* level.

I am always intrigued when I see that sometimes, a single answer – right or wrong – on an achievement test can change percentiles quite significantly (which is also an issue with some neuropsychological tests). Therefore, it is important to rely on the judgment of an experienced neuropsychologist to properly understand what scores actually mean, and not to take individual scores and percentiles at face value.

I close by emphasizing that IQ and achievement tests are integral to evaluations and serve two purposes – identifying ability, and measuring current achievement. They have their flaws and caveats, but ultimately they can provide considerable insight on how your child is functioning, particularly within an academic environment. The next chapter will cover the underlying aspects of cognition that influence both IQ and achievement tests – the neuropsychological domains.

FOOTNOTE 1

One of the most striking examples of environment influencing test performance is stereotype threat. Stereotype threat is a topic in social psychology that looks at people's behavior when they feel at risk of conforming to a particular stereotype. For example, the false belief that African Americans score lower on IQ tests can actually result in lower scores. Numerous studies have demonstrated that when African American children are exposed to a stereotype threat, they underperform compared to other African American children who do not experience the threat. Chapter 6 describes further examples of the impact of culture on cognition.

FOOTNOTE 2

Most modern IQ tests assess very specific abilities that include vocabulary, verbal reasoning, visual reasoning, visual-spatial abilities, abstract thinking, working memory, arithmetic, and processing speed. Aside from the fact that some of these abilities are directly affected by learning and attentional difficulties (artificially lowering the FSIQ), they do not capture all aspects of cognition. For example, children raised in a largely outdoor environment might have less use for solving block puzzles but instead need to identify plants and animals. They may need to develop better physical coordination at a younger age. Many theorists have outlined multiple systems of intelligence, with some (e.g. Howard Gardner) purporting that there may be a dozen or more worth considering including musical, artistic, and interpersonal intelligences.

FOOTNOTE 3

Social/emotional intelligence has attracted considerable attention in both the business and the school environment. The literature on the so-called EQ quotient is mixed – while studies do establish that high EQ can predict numerous desirable outcomes, there is controversy on what EQ is, and how it might be measured. Regardless, there is little debate that children on the autistic spectrum scale typically struggle in social environments. A subset of these children that show normal or even above average intelligence in some areas was previously referred to as "Asperger's syndrome" although this term has officially been dropped in favor of a spectrum model. Chapter 5 further explores EQ while Chapter 10 covers the autistic spectrum disorders.

FOOTNOTE 4

Readers of this chapter should immediately recognize that IQ tests are not truly "aptitude" tests, such that they do not *only* capture innate biological traits of intelligence. The mere fact that many IQ tests incorporate aspects of vocabulary and arithmetic should clue readers in to the fact that those who are raised in academically enriched environments are more likely to do well on these tests. There remains debate on which individual subtests are more robust to predisposed intellect and which are more influenced by culture and environment, but regardless, all these subtests are still merged into their respective indexes and the full scale IQ. Therefore, IQ tests represent both a combination of "biological" intelligence and environmental factors such as the quality of the child's education.

FOOTNOTE 5

A standard deviation is the average deviation any given score is expected to have from the mean. Assuming a normal distribution, if a mean is 10 with a standard deviation of 3, we know that on average, a random score selected from this sample will be between 7-13 points. This can directly be converted to percentiles; in a normal curve, 68% of scores are one standard deviation from the mean while 95% are two standard deviations. This is the basis by which percentiles are calculated.

FOOTNOTE 6

The IQ-achievement discrepancy model is attractive in its simplicity and perceived face value, but ultimately is not an optimal method of diagnosis. First of all, the need for a discrepancy score of a sufficient interval (usually two standard deviations) makes it more difficult for children with lower IQ scores to meet criteria – their achievement scores have that much further to fall! Furthermore, IQ and achievement scores are not completely reliable (i.e. scores will vary from assessment to assessment) and scores will vary from assessment to assessment. When two scores are not fully reliable, their numeral difference will be even less reliable (just imagine trying to calculate how much your child grew last year from two rulers that arbitrarily shift their lengths over time). Perhaps most importantly, research has demonstrated that there is little indication that the discrepancy model can accurately identify children with known learning disabilities that interfere with their classroom performance.

FOOTNOTE 7

There remains debate on whether learning disabilities are wholly "medical" (i.e. biological in origin) or societal. Support for the former includes family history of learning disabilities and some evidence of neurological correlates with certain disorders. However, and as mentioned, disabilities must always be identified by their actual dysfunction in the real world, not on test scores and so we must factor in how well a child is functioning in an actual school and general community Many professionals acknowledge that several learning disabilities emerge because of the cultural expectations of the Western academic world, which has become increasingly rigorous and competitive in the upper echelons. Chapter 10 provides further detail on the types, outcomes, and controversies of some of the most frequent learning disabilities.

CHAPTER 5

Neuropsychology Domains

Attention, processing speed, language, memory, visual-spatial skills, executive functioning, motor skills, social cognition. This chapter breaks down each of these terms and their potential significance.

While most psychological evaluations will include IQ and achievement scores, additional cognitive testing is the specialty of the neuropsychologist. Neuropsychological tests are designed to measure specific brain–behavior functions. While IQ tests are often concerned with a general "IQ" score, neuropsychological tests directly map onto different areas of the brain (see footnote 1). Standardized scores and percentiles are still examined, but patterns of scores, rather than any single score, are interpreted to explain cognition and behavior.

Neuropsychological tests measure a broad range of abilities that impact behavior, and therefore are quite sensitive to general dysfunction. However, they do not precisely measure a specific ability. For example, an executive functioning test will often indirectly examine the abilities of attention, processing speed, motor control, and other domains. This overlap must be considering when interpreting scores. Did a child perform poorly on a visual–spatial test solely because of a visual-spatial deficit, or is there a more general visual memory or fine motor weakness? These must be considered alongside other factors like perception, motivation, and mood.

Despite this overlap, tests can be grouped into domains with some reliability. People often perform poorly within some domains and much better on others, which can yield a pattern of scores that can highlight your child's strengths and weaknesses. Let's examine these domains a bit more closely.

Attention

Casey was diagnosed with an attention/deficit hyperactivity disorder. This was no surprise to her parents, who were long aware that she was absent minded and forgetful. Recently, her teacher expressed concerns about her homework, which is turned in late and sometimes not at all. When looking through Casey's report, her parents are surprised to see that she performed quite well on some attention tests, called "brief attentional tests," and poorly on a "sustained attention" test. In addition, the term "working memory" was sometimes used in the report when describing their daughter's attentional abilities.

Attention is a multifaceted aspect of cognition. It refers to our ability to attend to certain information while filtering out other information. During the evaluation we are usually concerned with explicit, conscious aspects of attention; namely, the ability to consciously focus on a target while ignoring other distractors, and then consolidating that information for future use. Neuropsychologists test attention with a number of tests that include digit spans (saying numbers that have to be repeated backwards and forwards), mental arithmetic, and the continuous performance tests, which involve staring at a computer for an extended period of time while looking for target stimuli (see footnote 2).

These tests are often sensitive to children who have trouble paying attention, but some things must be considered. First of all, an evaluation is (usually) a novel process and so sometimes children will attend very well to this strange adult who is paying *them* attention and do quite well on some of the tests. Second, children with attentional problems can often focus for brief periods of time, and so they can perform well on brief tests of attention. Sometimes these tests are explicitly referred to as "brief" attention tests, to distinguish them from "sustained attention" tests. The latter refers to tests that require concentration for extended periods of time and are often more sensitive to children who cannot sit still for very long.

Given that attention tests are given both in brief and longer intervals during an evaluation, then how might these translate towards behavior outside of the evaluation? As stated, children are sometimes initially quite interested in the evaluation, which can hide attentional problems. Some smarter children with ADHD might even remain invested for longer periods of time. Perhaps one of the best tests of attention is the evaluation itself. Nearly all children will grow restless and fidgety as time passes, but the speed at which they lose concentration can be critical information regarding attentional problems. We might expect a five-year-old to get bored 30 minutes into an evaluation, less so a twelve-year-old, particularly when this twelve-year-old is expected to sit for an hour at a time in class.

Some children favor visual information over auditory information and may do better on a visual attention test. This auditory/visual distinguish is often used with memory tests as well. "Working memory," is a complex construct that is tied with attention, memory, and executive functioning. Briefly, working memory refers to the conscious *manipulation* of information in short-term storage. Rather than simply saying a sequence of numbers back at the examiner, a child might have to reverse the order, or conduct some mental computations first. Working memory is very important for successful academic performance and is often weak in children with learning difficulties.

Finally, it might surprise parents to learn that neurocognitive tests of attention are not necessary for an ADHD diagnosis. Chapter 10 goes into more detail but ultimately, ADHD is a behavioral diagnosis. The reports of parents and teachers are essential for making a formal diagnosis, with the testing often serving to supplement in identifying learning styles and possible learning/cognitive disorders.

Processing Speed

Roger was always known as a quick thinker. Even at a young age he would surprise adults with his wit. In elementary school he was the first to finish assignments and be on the playground. Homework rarely took him more than fifteen to thirty minutes, in contrast with other parents' complaints about how long their children spent on homework. However, by high school even Roger was showing some struggles. He still finished assignments quickly, but his grades on tests were dropping from As to Bs. He would start studying for hours the night before a test, now blending in more with his slower peers, and yet still make careless mistakes.

Processing speed, or the speed at which your child can process information in a meaningful and accurate way, is an important aspect of the evaluation. Some children, like Roger, are naturally fast, but at times can become careless due to their speed. Other children might be quite intelligent but are hindered by a processing speed that is slower than what their intelligence would suggest. There are many things that can affect processing speed, which is why it is crucial to evaluate it using many different tests and modalities. Some tests rely on simple cancellation or sequencing tests, while others are more involved and require coding skills, or academic abilities.

Children who perform slowly on such tests do so for a number of reasons. Sometimes, children's processing speed might be normal but due to anxiety or mental fatigue, they are slow on these timed tests. It may relate to a fine motor or visual perception impairment, although other tests are usually administered to rule these out. Some forms of ADHD are linked to slowed processing speed due to poor concentration (see footnote 3). More serious conditions that involve brain injury almost invariably result in slowed processing. In this manner, processing speed can be viewed as a general barometer of brain health – when everything is working well, it should be normal or even fast (and accurate). When something affects the brain, processing speed often takes the first "hit."

I would like to emphasize that a slower response style does *not* mean your child has a brain injury. While brain injury almost invariably results in slowed processing speed, the reverse isn't true; there are many reasons why your child might be slower than average. Ruling out mood, learning, attentional, or motivation issues, slowed processing speed is sometimes just a normal variation in functioning. Your child may simply prefer to favor accuracy over speed, and think carefully (as in the gears grind finely, yet slowly) on tests. Knowing this can provide insight into your child's cognitive style, and perhaps even raise the possibility for accommodations that will assist during testing.

Language

Martin was referred for testing because he did not seem able to process information in class. Teachers would provide him instructions and he would just sit there with a confused look on his face. Curiously, he did much better on the playground and was often the captain of the various games children played during recess. There was a concern that he might have an attentional disorder, or he might simply be willful and noncompliant in school. Instead, he was diagnosed with a receptive language disorder; it wasn't that Martin was inattentive – he was attentive, but he simply couldn't understand what was expected of him.

Language is a complex system. It can be divided into expressive and receptive domains, although there are much finer distinctions that sometimes have to be assessed (see footnote 4). Expressive language refers to the ability to express thoughts, either verbally or through other means, such as written language. Receptive language refers to both auditory and reading comprehension. Sometimes children struggle in one specific area, while others have more global language issues that must be addressed.

When the issue is more expressive, children might have trouble getting words out or finding the right thing to say or write. Their memory for verbal material might be affected because they are less comfortable attending to language. Their vocabulary might be lower than expected. Sometimes expressive language disorders are the primarily explanation for a disorder of written expression. In contrast, receptive language issues relate to processing what others say or what is written. This can sometimes translate as a reading disorder. Some children are mistakenly diagnosed with an attentional disorder due to the superficial appearance that they are not paying attention, when in reality they just aren't comprehending information.

Some children struggle in more specific, isolated areas. Stuttering, lisping, slurred speech, among others fall under the umbrella of "communication disorders" without necessarily overlapping with an expressive or receptive delay. Sometimes, the cause is more motoric in nature. Chapter 10 provides more information about communication disorders.

Memory

Memory is one of the most important aspects of human consciousness — after all, what aspect of our self-awareness isn't linked to past knowledge? Memory concerns are usually more prevalent in older individuals, particularly the elderly who may be developing dementia. In children, memory is typically not impaired at a significant level unless there is neurological explanation. However, memory tests can still be useful in identifying how a particular child processes information.

When the neuropsychologist goes over Sandy's report, she emphasizes that Sandy's memory system is likely fine, but she does not necessarily use the best strategies to learn new information. The doctor highlights this based on Sandy's performance across several tests. On a list learning test, in which Sandy had to memorize a list over five trials, her performance was relatively flat. Inspection of items revealed that she didn't really use any strategies to remember words, such as grouping them into categories (like clothing or food). In contrast, Sandy did quite well on a story memory test in which the "strategy" was already presented to her, in the form of a logical and interesting story. She also performed quite well on a visual test for faces, which was interesting for her, and poorly on a memory test of abstract images. The neuropsychologist concluded that some of Sandy's learning problems in the classes can be linked to attentional and executive issues, which in turn impact her ability to remember some things as efficiently as other things.

Generally, memory is assessed for both short-term (i.e. 30 seconds) and long-term (i.e. 20-30 minutes) recall. Recognition, or the ability to identify previously learned information without recalling it on your own, is also tested. Verbal and visual memory are often looked at – it's common that children may prefer one learning style over another. These scores can often have direct application in the classroom; for example, if a child is shown to prefer auditory verbal information over visual cues, lessons can be tailored to capitalize on this strength.

The memory system is much more complex than what is described here, but for the typical school-aged child, memory should generally align with overall intellectual abilities unless there is a suspected attentional or cognitive disorder. In many cases, issues with attention, concentration, and executive functioning better explain any memory issues, although as stated earlier, neurological conditions can also directly affect memory. What is sometimes neglected is the fact that emotional health can impact memory as well. This is quite common in the elderly (see footnote 5) but can also be a factor with children and adolescents. In some cases, poor performance on memory tests might actually be best explained by depression and/or anxiety.

Visual-spatial Abilities

Visual-spatial abilities refer to visual abilities that generally involve shapes and images. I hesitate to use the term "nonverbal" here as many visual learners still verbalize visual information to assist with learning. After all, a square is called a square, not a triangle. Sometimes, visual-spatial skills are assessed alongside visual-motor abilities, which involve physically drawing or rotating shapes to fit a pattern.

Behaviorally, visual-spatial weaknesses might show through poorer coordination, difficulties with abstract images and art, and trouble with directions. Sometimes this is expressed through poor handwriting and in math class through difficulties in geometry and coordinates. More global weaknesses might reflect a developmental coordination disorder or a nonverbal learning disorder, the latter which is also associated with poorer social skills due to difficulties in reading body language. Conversely, children with strengths in visual-spatial skills often excel in the arts and abstract thinking. Such children may be more inclined to pursue more visually oriented careers, such as those in mechanical engineering, architecture, or graphic design.

Executive Functioning

Executive functioning has received increasing attention in the general population. This construct is commonly affected in children with ADHD or neurological injury and often is behaviorally expressed through learning difficulties as well as social and emotional issues. However, the concept of "executive functioning" remains a bit vague in what it exactly encompasses. Tests of executive functioning widely vary in modality and range from an abstract reasoning test, to a test where attention has to be switched between two competing objects, to a test of response inhibition, among others. Children and adults generally do well on some of these tests and not so well on others – so what exactly do these measures encompass?

Unlike memory, or attention, or some of the other domains, the link between executive functioning and what we perceive as human thought is less obvious, although still very much present. This construct perhaps first emerged from lesion studies, in which individuals who suffered blows to the front of the brain often had preserved memory, attention, and intelligence and yet were behaviorally very different from before (see footnote 6). Over time, tests were invented that were found to be sensitive to these lesions. These tests usually captured what might be thought of as "higher order abilities," or abilities that often are involved with regulation of thought and behavior.

Alex was diagnosed with ADHD, although in truth his attention to things can be quite good – particularly when he is interested in something. He might spend hours reading through manuals of computer science and easily can be engrossed in a video game. His attention does not really hold in the classroom, but it is other behaviors that concern his teachers. For example, he is impulsive and will often blurt out answers in class, even when they are obviously wrong. He is restless and fidgety and will get up and bother other children during study time. He cannot follow directions – when asked to do something that takes more than two steps or three minutes, he will lose focus and engage in another activity. Of note, Alex at times seems perplexed by his inability to stay on task. He is a sweet boy and wants to do well, and gets frustrated with himself almost as much as his parents and teachers.

Children who struggle with executive functioning are often hyper, impulsive, and have trouble staying on task. They might have trouble planning ahead, managing their time, and following multi-step procedures. In some cases, emotional outbursts and mood swings might be present. Other signs of executive dysfunction include concrete thinking (i.e. an inability to think things at an abstract level), repeating oneself over and over again (i.e. perseveration), difficulty adapting to new situations, and mental disorganization. Because executive functioning is the executive, or "CEO" part of the brain, difficulties in this can impact many other aspects of cognition including attention, working memory, long-term memory, and processing speed.

Executive functioning covers a whole range of different abilities, their common feature being that they are linked to the frontal lobes, which are the largest regions of gray matter in our brains. A comprehensive neuropsychological evaluation will cover all these abilities and provide a profile that is unique to your children. For example, a child might have good abstract thinking but poor mental flexibility, such that she cannot switch from one task to another without great effort. This might be accommodated by providing a schedule of the day to prepare her of her expectations, with less concern about her ability to problem-solve in class.

On another note, parents might note that several symptoms of executive dysfunction – such as poor planning and impulse control and hyperactivity, are "symptoms" that are present in many children – particularly those who are younger. Research has criticized the sensitivity of some executive tests in the very young. Executive functioning is often difficult to evaluate in children who are below 6 years of age, and even still a challenge until about age 8, because young children simply haven't developed many executive abilities up until this age. This results in problems with test norms. "Poor" performance might translate as "average" performance because most young children will perform pretty poorly on a specific test. However, young children with real executive difficulties will often act unusually disruptive in school and home and so issues related to ADHD or other conditions can still be assessed.

Motor Skills

Motor skills can be roughly divided into gross motor skills, or coordination of the whole body for running, jumping, and other movements, and fine motor skills, or dexterity of the fingers for writing, tying shoelaces, and other small movements. Children may have difficulty with one, the other, or both and testing can identify these weaknesses. Usually, gross motor issues are evident just by asking a child to walk or run, or catch a ball. Grip strength tests can be used to measure upper body strength. Fine motor skills can be examined by watching how the child writes or tries to tie shoelaces, although more precise measures are available.

Poor motor skills might affect a child's ability to write, draw, or engage in other classroom activities. They can impact a child's athleticism and lead to social and emotional difficulties. Children develop these skills at different rates so if your child is behind, it may represent a temporary setback. However, neurological conditions can affect the motor system as well. A developmental coordination disorder, which is discussed in Chapter 10, is often characterized by motor and visual-spatial difficulties. In addition, neurological injuries that affect one side of the brain might impact the motor system of the opposite side of the body – therefore, tests of gross and fine motor ability might be sensitive to general brain dysfunction that is present in just one of the hemispheres.

Social Cognition

On paper, Mira is a stellar student. She received all As in her seventh grade class and won multiple awards and recognitions. And yet, Mira is still struggles in school. Her struggles are more of a social nature – although she gets along fine with her parents and younger siblings, she is somewhat of a social outcast. Other girls don't seem to want to talk to her and one particular girl has started teasing Mira. Mira's response to these is generally to say offbeat things that only provoke further teasing. Her only friend is a childhood girlfriend outside of school, but this friend shares many of her eclectic interests. Mira is somewhat annoyed by her lack of friends at school but also seems fairly content with herself, aside from teasing. Her parents have some concerns about her ability to thrive in high school and decide to seek an evaluation.

Social cognition is an aspect of cognition dedicated to processing and communicating social information in an adaptive way. Like executive functioning, it is a somewhat vague construct that is more obvious when it is absent rather than when it is working well. Children and adults with social cognitive issues often have trouble recognizing emotions (both visual and prosodic), understanding social conventions and customs, and emphasizing with what other people are thinking and feeling (e.g. theory of mind). Literature has demonstrated that in the adult world, social cognition is as important if not more so for success in many enterprises, and so this area has been attracting increasing attention.

In my opinion, social cognition remains a difficult construct to assess at this time. There exist some tests that are designed to measure it, either through emotional recognition or theory of mind games (e.g. "What is that girl thinking in this picture? Why?)" However, such tests rarely translate well to the complex social milieu of the real world. Many children with social difficulties actually do well on these tests, and children with no social difficulties might perform poorer for other reasons, such as attentional difficulties. Furthermore, culture plays a tremendous role in what is socially appropriate and what is not. It may be that one's flexibility and adaptability to social situations is a useful metric to social cognition, although it might be argued that executive functioning captures this. Indeed, many children with social problems do poorer on executive functioning tests, rather than the purposed social cognition tests. Additional social functioning measures can be obtained through self and other-report scales, as well as behavioral observations from the neuropsychologist.

Regardless of how it is assessed, social cognition is certainly an area of clinical interest. Parents may be concerned that their child's social needs may not be fulfilled, or that they may be at risk for future emotional concerns. Fortunately, there are many resources available aimed at improving social functioning. Chapter 10, which covers the autistic spectrum disorders, will cover this in more depth.

Report Measures

The above measures are largely performance based, such that they measure your child's skills using specific tests of ability. However, neurocognitive domains can also be assessed through self and other-report measures. These measures are essentially rating scales in which parents, teachers, and sometimes the child will rate various abilities. Report measures provide an essential dimension to the evaluation and are often used to supplement formal measures of executive functioning and social cognition. For example, a child might report that he or she is very organized but this is not congruent with the teacher-report measures or the neurocognitive tests. Disparities between test scores and report scores can provide additional insight on how different people perceive the child's abilities. Finally, report forms are a common method of assessing emotional functioning, which will be covered in the next chapter.

FOOTNOTE 1

Initially, it was hoped that tests would look at very specific locations of the brain – here is the "verbal memory" part of the brain, or the "sustained attention" part of the brain. With some possible exceptions in the language and motor systems, this really does not apply. However, neuroimaging studies have validated that tests do measure brain functions, some which are localized to a few regions and others that reflect connectivity among different regions. More precise measures do exist and are often used in experimental studies. However, these very precise laboratory measures are less useful in predicting outcomes of actual patients.

FOOTNOTE 2

Continuous performance tests are tests of sustained attention in which patients have to stare at a screen for a prolonged period of time and push a button whenever they see a target item, while refraining from pushing the button at non-target items. These can be useful for detecting attentional issues and some research confirms that these tests are sensitive to children with ADHD. However, as mentioned above, some children with attentional problems can maintain focus in certain situations, and the computer "game" presentation of a continuous performance test might be one of them. Therefore, these tests alone are not sufficient for detecting attentional problems and should also be used alongside other tests and a comprehensive interview, report forms, and behavioral observations.

FOOTNOTE 3

ADHD can be subdivided into the primarily inattentive subtype, or the combined inattentive/hyperactive subtype (a third type, the primarily hyperactive subtype, is less common). Children with the inattentive subtype generally do not have the same behavioral issues as those with the combined subtype – they are less disruptive and impulsive and often sit quietly in class. However, just because they are quiet does not mean they are focusing – such children often have trouble remembering what they learned and applying it to their work. Cognitively, many children with the inattentive subtype will perform quite slowly on processing speed tests, due to mental sluggishness and poor concentration. Of interest, it is suspected that many girls with the inattentive subtype go undiagnosed because they usually attract less attention than children with the combined subtype.

FOOTNOTE 4

The language system is quite complex but its associated brain regions are well-mapped out. Typically, the dominant hemisphere holds the language network. For right-handed people, this is the left hemisphere while left-handed people might have it in the right or left hemisphere. Broca's area is in the frontal cortex and is linked with expressive language, while Wernicke's area is in the temporal cortex and is linked with receptive language. Linking the two regions is the arcuate fasciculus, a bundle of white matter tracts that is linked with speech repetition.

FOOTNOTE 5

Pseudodementia is a term used to characterize individuals who display some signs of dementia, including memory loss and confusion, yet do not actually have any neurological signs of deterioration. Rather, the best explanation offered in this case is a psychiatric etiology such as depression or a related mood disorder. While it would be quite unusual to see a child with pseudodementia, children who are dealing with psychological or psychiatric conditions often experience subjective cognitive changes, such as attentional problems or memory loss.

FOOTNOTE 6

One notable case study was that of Phineas Gage, a railroad worker in the 19th century. While blasting rock to make way for a railway, an accidental blast fired the tampering iron through the frontal lobes of his brain. To everyone's surprise, he quickly regained consciousness and was able to walk and speak. He made a slow but steady recovery and eventually was discharged from the doctor. However, noted behavioral and personality changes were recorded including lewd behavior, impulsivity, and disorganization; Gage was noted to be "fitful, irreverent...capricious and vacillating" in stark contrast to his pre-injury state. Reports of his personality changes may have been exaggerated over time, but he clearly exhibited some of the behavioral symptoms of frontal lobe dysfunction.

CHAPTER 6

Emotional Health

Our consciousness derives from the complex interplay between cognition and emotion. Disentangling what is psychological and what is neurological is one of the most challenging jobs of the neuropsychologist.

Neuropsychologists are first and foremost, psychologists. Psychologists are trained to assess and treat mental health disorders. While neuropsychologists have specialized training in the assessment of neurological and neurodevelopmental disorders, they always must factor in the psychological aspects of functioning. Numerous case studies have demonstrated the powerful effect that one's mental state can have on behavior, with psychological disorders mimicking actual medical conditions in more extreme cases (see footnote 1). It goes without saying that your child's mood will influence his or her cognitive performance, including performance on neuropsychological tests.

Dr. Sweet observes that her patient, a twelve-year old girl, appears lethargic and absent minded. Her performance on an initial IQ battery is not great – particularly on timed tests where she is sluggish and distracted. Her parents mentioned that their daughter has been having a "rough" time. Dr. Sweet puts away the tests and begins to talk to the girl. Over time, she learns that she is sad because of her grandmother's recent passing, and cruel comments about her grandmother's death from some boys at school. It becomes apparent that her sadness goes beyond these recent stressors and she has had transient thoughts of suicide for the past year. Upon further evaluation, Dr. Sweet determines that her patient is suffering a major depressive episode. Cognitive testing is set aside for the moment in lieu of developing an intervention plan.

As stated, there are many factors that can influence test performance - depression and anxiety being chief among them. Sometimes, a child will be referred for assessment due to a suspected learning or attentional issue, only to discover that a mood or anxiety disorder is responsible for their difficulties. In some cases, as observed above, the severity of the disorder is enough that further cognitive testing is not indicated, as results will not accurately reflect the child's true potential.

How do emotional states affect testing? The answer is not too difficult if you view it through a behavioral lens – what does someone with depression look like? Lethargic, sad, apathetic, and withdrawn might be some words that come to mind. Apply these terms to testing and you might see that depressed individuals often perform quite slowly on tests. Therefore, tests of attention and processing speed are often impacted. Excess anxiety can make you feel hypervigilant and tense – which can also influence attention and concentration. Anxiety can also make individuals impulsive or careless, such that they respond too quickly on test items or rush through things just to get them done. At the same time, anxiety may make children reluctant to respond to questions due to a fear of getting items wrong. Such a "perfectionist" approach can generalize to the classroom, where such children may appear well-behaved and quiet but at the expense of excess anxiety in participating.

Unlike cognitive testing, which is primarily performance-based with some parent and self-report measures used to supplement results, emotional states are assessed through report measures, interviews, and behavioral observations during the evaluation. Reporting your child's functioning on a parent-report scale is an indispensable portion of the evaluation. Many self, parent, and teacher-report scales are available and many are quite comprehensive. Psychologists are also aware of the diagnostic criteria of various conditions and so can often come to a diagnosis by asking and looking for specific symptoms, as well as ascertaining their severity and duration.

> *Robert is a nine-year old boy whose mother passed away last year. His father brings him in for an evaluation because of his poor reading and spelling. Robert is friendly and polite and engages with the examiner, although he becomes distracted and irritable at times. His father notes that he was not like this before his mother died. The examiner decides to administer some additional measures to assess Robert's internal state. He provides Robert a sentence completion test, and asks him to describe ambiguous pictures of people. Through this, he learns that Robert has a lot of underlying anger and aggression and he feels frustrated with his dad and the new woman he has just started seeing.*

While self-report measures can be useful, they are generally not appropriate for younger children or any child who is not particularly forthcoming. Projective measures are tests that are helpful in identifying the child's mood, thoughts, and motives by serving as conduits that allow children to express themselves in an abstract way that feels safer to them. Sandplay is a type of projective testing that can be particularly useful for nonverbal children (e.g. very young children, and those on the autistic spectrum scale). Rather than dialogue, symbolic play is used to express one's internal state.

Projective testing is often helpful simply because children do not express depression and anxiety in the same way as adults. Depression may be masked as irritability, or defiance, or physical symptoms like stomach pain or headaches. Children may not yet have developed the vocabulary or understanding of their mood states to sufficiently communicate to their parents – and some children may not feel comfortable doing so even if they could. It is also important to know that these conditions can manifest in different ways, both between children and sometimes within the same child at different times of his or her life.

> *Dr. Murphy holds an interview with Paul's mother and learns that Paul's father is in London for six months on a work contract. Paul's older brother is in the Marines and Paul looks very much up to his brother. He attends a public school and regularly goes to church, but does not get along with the children at either setting. He gets along better with the kids in his volleyball team and is a strong athlete there. However, Paul's mother expressed concern about taking her son to future games because of her schedule and his father's absence. Furthermore, Paul has been conflicting with his math teacher and has gotten three detentions this year alone, something that has not happened before. Of note, his best friend recently was diagnosed with leukemia and Paul has been having trouble dealing with this.*

A proper evaluation has to take in context the family, community, and culture of the child in explaining what is going on. No psychological or cognitive test will ever be able to address the types of questions that a comprehensive interview can. In some ways, a psychologist acts like a detective – there are facts and opinions presented to the examiner, who then relies on his or her knowledge about how these might relate to each other as well as to the presenting problem. Paul has a number of things going on – some more stressful than others, but all relevant and important to follow up on, even if we don't yet know what his presenting issue might be. If the information is not comprehensive enough, then a crucial detail (such as Paul's friend's illness) might be ignored, and potential diagnoses (e.g. depression) might be made without understanding the full context.

Elliot's parents are flummoxed by their son's recent changes. Soon after his eighteenth birthday, Elliot began to act increasingly erratic and withdrawn. He would spend hours in his room listening to music and watching the same movie over and over again. He broke up with his girlfriend of two years with little explanation and began to skip showering unless explicitly told to by his parents. Although he was recently accepted into a competitive university, his parents wonder if he can make the transition to college in his current state. His pediatrician finds nothing medically wrong with him and so refers him to a psychiatrist for depression. The psychiatrist determines that Elliot may actually have some early signs of psychosis and sends him to a neuropsychologist for cognitive testing. The results of the test reveal some cognitive deficits, which can happen in the early stages of schizophrenia. Elliot is immediately put on an antipsychotic regime to prevent a full break from occurring.

Often, depression and/or anxiety are the primary factors to consider during an evaluation. Sometimes, however, other conditions may be present. Children who experience trauma may develop post-traumatic stress disorder, which can lead to very real cognitive and learning delays. Obsessive-compulsive disorder is a form of anxiety typified by excessive obsessions and subsequent compulsions designed to reduce anxiety; OCD has also been linked with cognitive impairment (see footnote 2). Adolescents and young adults may also develop psychiatric conditions such as bipolar disorder and schizophrenia. Most families will not have to worry about either condition, which affect 1-2 out of 100 individuals. However, rates of these illnesses are higher when there is a family history and in such cases, early intervention is critical to ensure proper treatments are put into place (see footnote 3). While these illnesses are primarily treated through medication and supportive therapy, sometimes a neuropsychologist is enlisted to track changes in cognition that may occur alongside treatment.

Other psychological disorders are identified primarily by their externalizing features. Oppositional defiant disorder is diagnosed when children display a persistent pattern of argumentative and defiant behavior over six months. Such children are irritable and angry and are vindictive towards adults and their peers. A more serious externalizing condition is conduct disorder, in which children engage in destructive and harmful acts towards others. Conduct disorder may often transfer into adult antisocial personality disorder (see footnote 4) if left untreated. Both conditions are diagnosable independent of a neuropsychological evaluation but there are often cognitive and learning difficulties that may underlie the behaviors. For example, youth with conduct disorder often have impairments in executive functioning which can contribute to their impulsive and hostile acts. Substance use, which such youth often engage in, can also contribute to cognitive issues. Both conditions are also frequently associated with depression and other mood disturbances and so assessment of emotional functioning is crucial in tailoring a treatment plan.

As the new kid at school, Sarah initially had a difficult time adjusting to the ninth grade. This all changed after she met Beth and Margaret, two of the more popular girls who took her under their wing. At first her parents were delighted that their daughter was fitting in. However, some cracks started to emerge as the year progressed. Sarah was spending more time out than on her studies and her mid-semester grades began to reflect this – normally a straight A student, she obtained a B- in English class. When asked, Sarah said that she was struggling with the material and that "Nothing was coming to mind" on her tests. She added that she was having trouble focusing in her classes and that other students seemed to get the material much faster than she. Emotionally, their previously cheerful and open daughter began to grow more reserved. She would hide in her room when talking to her friends and be vague about where she was going out. One night she came home two hours past curfew and there was the distinct smell of alcohol on her breath.

Is Sarah going through the normal struggles of adolescence or is there something more going on? What about her grades – perhaps she has an undiagnosed learning or attentional condition? Maybe she is depressed, or maybe she is simply caught up with the wrong crowd. It is difficult to say with certainty what the next step might be, but at the very least, a consultation with the school is warranted. By hearing the teachers' input, it may be easier to determine whether a follow up evaluation might identify what exactly is going on.

Emotional health is part and parcel of cognitive (and overall) health, and it cannot be neglected. From a testing standpoint, youth with psychological illnesses may underperform on neuropsychological tests, and so actual learning and cognitive disorders might be masked. At the same time, some mental health conditions directly result in cognitive impairments, while others arise because of cognitive difficulties. As such, a comprehensive assessment of cognitive and emotional states, as well as the larger environment in which your child functions, is essential in coming up with an accurate diagnosis and treatment plan.

FOOTNOTE 1

Somatoform disorders refer to mental illnesses that result in physical symptoms, including pain and stomach problems. In children, these disorders are persistent and chronic over time – therefore, a child who occasionally stays home from school due to a vague stomach complaint would not qualify for this diagnosis. For a diagnosis to be made, the symptoms must significantly interfere with the child's life. Such children are often seen more in medical rather than mental health settings due to the nature of the complaints. However, the origin of these disorders almost invariably relate to some kind of psychological distress. Illustrative of this, children who are victims of abuse and trauma often develop somatoform disorders, although not all children with somatoform disorders are such victims.

FOOTNOTE 2

PTSD refers to longstanding psychological trauma due to an environmental event. The chronic stress associated with the trauma can have actual neurological impact on the brain and result in cognitive impairments in attention, memory, and executive functioning. OCD also is linked with deficits in executive functioning, which may contribute to the persistent and pervasive thoughts that characterize the condition. Other anxiety disorders, such as social phobia and generalized anxiety, can impact test performance but are less strongly linked to actual cognitive impairments inherent of the conditions themselves.

FOOTNOTE 3

Individuals who have psychosis often have what is called the prodromal period of psychosis, in which their behavior and thoughts become altered, but not to the level of a full psychotic break. Schizophrenia and other psychotic illnesses typically manifest during the late teens and early twenties for men and mid-twenties for women. There is currently an enormous interest in better identifying individuals who are at risk for transitioning to psychosis, as the research proves that catching it earlier ultimately leads to better long-term outcomes.

FOOTNOTE 4

Personality disorders refer to pervasive and maladaptive patterns of functioning that are believed to relate to innate, stable personality traits. Antisocial personality disorder, for example, is a diagnosis given to individuals who have low empathy, repeatedly disregard and violate the rights of others, and often have an extensive criminal history. As personality forms up through the mid-twenties, children and adolescents are still at a point where their personality can be influenced and shaped (although adult personalities can also change, it is considerably harder to do so). This is in part the reason why interventions are crucial to implement early on, so that they can prevent the emergence of dysfunctional behaviors, thoughts, and mood states that can influence someone for the rest of his or her life.

CHAPTER 7

Cultural Factors

This chapter reviews the effects that cross-cultural and within-cultural practices can have on the assessment process.

In the previous chapter, I describe how the environment is critical to integrate into the evaluation. One of the most important environmental factors to consider is the child's cultural background – the practices, beliefs, and behaviors that have shaped the child as well as other children and adults around him/her. To say it simply, culture is *everywhere* (see footnote 1). It is not something to consider only when working with someone from a different ethnic background, nor is it (only) an academic pursuit that is best left to the experts and textbooks.

Bill is a twenty-five-year-old doctoral student who is studying to be a child neuropsychologist. He comes an upper-middle class family in Chicago. His parents are married and send him care packages every few months. Just before today's patient, he learns from his mother that his older sister is pregnant and that the whole family is getting together in two months for a pre-wedding celebration. Delighted and in a great mood, he welcomes the new family in. The interview with the mother goes reasonably well and then Bill begins to interview the child, a ten-year old boy with the same eye and hair color as Bill. He feels an immediate connection with the boy. He asks him how his mom and dad are doing. When the boy hesitates, Bill rushes in and says, "I bet you love them a lot, don't you?"

The first vignette is not an example of ethnicity, but of privilege. Bill is fortunate to come from a well-loved and strong family. Unfortunately, in this case he is quick to project his circumstances onto a patient. We do not know this boy's relationship with his parents, but Bill has made up his mind and might subsequently miss critical information – for example, perhaps the boy is having conflict with his mother and this is contributing to his school withdrawal. In a somewhat ironic twist, Bill's oversight in part occurs because he feels too *much* kinship with the boy – if the boy looked differently or came from another background, he might not have been so quick to make this error.

You might wonder whose job it is to worry about cultural issues. As the client, it is fair to place the burden on the neuropsychologist to ensure that he or she uses the best cultural practices at hand in providing a fair evaluation. With that said, it can be helpful to know some of the common factors that a neuropsychologist might consider during an evaluation just for your own understanding of the process. Therefore, this chapter will first review some aspects of cultural neuropsychology that clinicians should know, and then will close with aspects that may be more relevant for you and your child.

Javier and Lisette are first-generation Mexican Americans. Their son, Carlos, has been undergoing evaluation for the past two weeks. The doctor has been very professional but there have been some frustrations. For example, Lisette's mother, who lives at home and has been with Carlos since he was a baby, wants to participate in the evaluation but she does not speak English, while the doctor does not speak Spanish. Javier's own English is passable but sometimes he is unsure if he is fully communicating everything he wants to convey to the doctor. However, he is reluctant to voice his concerns as it was difficult to secure this appointment in the first place, and both parents are hopeful that they finally may obtain some answers about their son.

Language fluency plays a significant role in the evaluation. It goes without saying that you must find a practitioner who can communicate in the same language as your child. When your child is bilingual, or if some of the people in the child's life cannot speak the same language, the issue is a bit murkier. In an ideal situation, bilingual children are assessed by bilingual neuropsychologists. This is more feasible in some cities than others depending on availability of doctors and the language in question. In the above vignette, there are some communication issues that might limit the richness of collateral interviews. Whether or not an outside referral is appropriate is most likely contingent on the availability of such referrals.

Some parents might consider using an interpreter during the evaluation. In general, the use of interpreters should be limited because much information can be lost in translation (see footnote 2). Test administrations should not rely on translators either, as this violates the standardized methods used when the data were collected. Interpreters should only be used in extraordinary circumstances in which a child speaks a language that is rare and no clinician can be found who can speak the same language.

Michael is a thirteen-year old boy undergoing evaluation for a cognitive deficit secondary to a medical condition. He is a second-generation Chinese American. His parents immigrated from Shenzhen in their early twenties and speak only some English. Michael grew up speaking English, Mandarin, and some Cantonese, the latter two which are primarily spoken within the home. His mother wants the evaluation completed while his father has little interest in the process. They secure a bilingual Mandarin/English neuropsychologist, Dr. Brown, who grew up in the United States. During the evaluation, Dr. Brown notes that Michael's parents live in a predominantly Chinese neighborhood in a city that has a fairly small and insular Chinese population. Michael attends a charter school with predominantly white and Asian American children and has had some trouble fitting in. He admits to Dr. Brown that he feels somewhat "different" from the other Asian American kids, who seem much more at ease intermixing with the white kids.

Acculturation refers to the degree someone integrates another culture's traits into their own culture. Testing itself is cultural, as some groups are more familiar with the concept of standardized testing than others. Differences in acculturation between parents and their children can lead to familial conflict that may be important for the neuropsychologist to assess. In the above vignette, Michael is not the only Asian child at school but he still feels a bit of an outcast compared to the other children, who (at least in his perspective) are more integrated into the mainstream culture.

Dr. Schmidt's patient is a nineteen-year old Japanese girl who grew up in the United States. This girl speaks English and Japanese and can communicate just fine in both languages. Dr. Schmidt, who does not speak Japanese, agrees to the evaluation although he has not worked with very many Asians before. He consults with a colleague and reads up on cultural characteristics of Japanese individuals. From his research he gleans that Japanese people may be less prone to verbally describe psychological distress. They may speak in a more indirect manner than people from the United States and may defer more to the doctor. While Japanese individuals are familiar with the concept of testing and particularly, standardized testing, they may be more reluctant to take risks on neuropsychological testing and avoid guessing, which can lower some scores. Armed with this new information, Dr. Schmidt welcomes the patient into his office with renewed confidence.

Is Dr. Schmidt now competent to see this Japanese girl or is he perhaps overestimating his abilities? Without prior experience, he likely is overestimating himself, which is even more of a concern if he is unaware of his bias. Clinicians who are aware of their limitations can approach an assessment more thoughtfully, or know to refer out if there are better resources available. Of note, this vignette highlights an example of cross-cultural work. Cross-cultural practices occur when someone of one culture works with someone from another culture. Traditionally, professionals become familiar with the practices, beliefs, and relevant characteristics of individuals from another group in order to better serve such individuals. In this sense, Dr. Schmidt did nothing particularly wrong. There is literature to support the above statements about the Japanese culture and some of this may factor into the assessment. However, some readers might observe that such blanket statements border on stereotyping. While it is fine to know some trends about people stemming from a certain background, it is dangerous to assume that a particular person of that background will invariably fit into that mold.

A personal criticism I have of cross-cultural practices is that it assumes culture can be packed into a neat "other" box that merits some consideration, but ultimately can be compartmentalized. It is archaic to think that you have to review specific trends of say, African American teenagers, and once you do you can simply apply those to your patient and move on. This ties with my initial statement that culture is in everything we do. Race and ethnicity are by far not the only cultural factors to consider. For example, a Caucasian man and an African American man who were raised in Boston in a similar neighborhood would have more in common with each other than the same African American man would with a black man living in Jamaica. Culture cannot be separated from human cognition and behavior, and so rather than thinking "cross-culturally," which sets a precedent for an "us" and "them," it is best to acknowledge the universal nature of cultural factors during the assessment.

Mira is a ten-year-old African American/Caucasian girl presenting for an evaluation. Her mind is a bit preoccupied by a recent incident in which her older cousin, who is black, made a comment that black people in general are "dumb." Mira never heard of such a belief before but now she had trouble shaking this thought. She has yet to bring it up to her parents but she secretly wondered if this might explain why she seemed to always work harder than her white friends at school. What was the purpose of this evaluation even for, she wonders? The well-intentioned neuropsychologist, who is white, smiled at Mira and gently informs her that these tests will assess her intelligence, academics, and memory. Mira's anxiety spikes to a new degree — suddenly she feels as if her cousin's words are about to come true.

Stereotype threat is the very real phenomenon in which people of a certain background may feel at risk of falling into a stereotype about their group. Numerous studies have demonstrated that this threat can affect minorities and lead to underperformance on IQ and achievement tests, particularly with African Americans (see footnote 3). Mira's neuropsychologist was careless in highlighting the intellectual aptitude portion of the exam, and Mira is now feeling added pressure based on her recent interaction with her cousin. Unfortunately, this can sometimes lead to a self-fulfilling prophecy in which she might underperform because she is now aware that "IQ" is on the line.

An additional consideration relates to the appropriateness of norms. Tests are normed on specific populations and so the percentiles that emerge really can only apply to these populations. For example, a child who grew up speaking Spanish and English in the United States may be better served with a Spanish adaptation of the test — but only if that test was normed on bilingual children in the United States. A substitute test that was normed in Spain would be problematic to administer in this child. Unfortunately, we are still in the developing stages of acquiring tests appropriate for bilingual children, or children from other countries and sometimes neuropsychologists will use whatever is on hand. While not ideal, useful information can still be obtained with the caveat that some of the exact scores and percentiles might not be as accurate as usual (see footnote 4).

As a parent, how might you use this information during an evaluation? First and foremost, it is important to ensure that cultural factors that you think are relevant are raised to the neuropsychologist. Family history, ethnic background, religious beliefs, it all applies. The more you disclose, the better we can fully understand the factors involved in the evaluation. I encourage you not to hide your own concerns about a cultural or language mismatch. You should always feel safe in disclosing such matters – in the event that you do not feel safe, it might be an indication to seek another professional. Maybe most importantly, it is important to try to view yourself and your child through a cultural lens. When disclosing information, think about your environment. What is the culture underlying your child's school? What cultural values are most important to you, and which of those do you try to impart to your child? By adapting a cultural lens in the manner that clinicians adapt, you will allow for a broader appreciation of how your child functions in his or her setting, and how this directly pertains to whatever concerns brought your family to the evaluation in the first place.

FOOTNOTE 1

When I say culture is everywhere, I do not mean it as a hyperbole. Think of a developing fetus. Nutrition, stress, and diseases all directly influence the initial development. This of course influences early childhood, as well as other factors such as access to healthcare and community services. These will have long term effects on cognitive and physical development and will interact with cultural values within the child's environment. Some cultures might emphasize community while others promote independence; some ascribe illness to weakness while others acknowledge its biological basis. All of this will all shape how your child experiences and expresses himself. Perhaps most fascinating is the study of epigenetics, or the shaping of the environment on an individual's very genetic makeup. While genes were once thought to be immutable at birth, it is now evident that stress, chemical agents, and other environmental factors can switch genes "on" or "off" and trigger new behaviors later in life.

FOOTNOTE 2

For a concrete example, consider a digit span test in which a series of numbers have to be attended to and recited back to the examiner. Children from Korean and Mandarin backgrounds will on average outperform children from English and Spanish backgrounds. This is simply due to the fact that the number of syllables that make up numbers are overall fewer in the former language, which eases working memory load. Vocabulary and list-learning tests also deal with this issue – some words are more familiar within the United States (e.g. "yoke") and would be foreign to someone hailing from a less agricultural nation. Even the direct translation of test instructions might lead to miscommunication; do the instructions of a block design test explicitly allow a child to self-correct, or is the implicit message that you only get one chance per trial?

FOOTNOTE 3

Stereotype threat is essentially caused by anxiety. Research suggests that individuals have increased stress, heightened self-monitoring of performance, and increased distractibility as they try to suppress negative thoughts and feelings. This all is counterproductive to optimal test testing and can result in underperformance. It is interesting to note that as stereotype threat is essentially a circumscribed form of test anxiety, it highlights the significant role that test anxiety in general can have on performance.

FOOTNOTE 4

The appropriateness of using tests on an individual outside of the normative group hinges on a number of factors, including the nature of the referral question, availability of appropriate norms (if they exist at all), and the training of the examiner. In general, when the purpose of the evaluation is to compare someone to others, norms are problematic as the percentiles are usually inaccurate. Gifted evaluations, for example, would not be an appropriate setting for non-normed tests. However, if the purpose is to identify individual strengths and weaknesses, then an evaluation *might* be appropriate. In such a case, the neuropsychologist would focus primarily on score differences within the child, rather than differences compared to other children. It might be possible, for example, to identify a visual-spatial deficit by comparing a patient's visual-spatial scores to his or her other cognitive domains. This deficit in turn may explain some of the academic struggles the child is experiencing.

CHAPTER 8

The Multidisciplinary Team

The neuropsychologist is just one part of a team of professionals, teachers, and parents who come together to help address a child in need. This chapter reviews who is on the team and how all the members interact in helping you and your child.

We are fortunate to live in a time where academic, cognitive, medical, and psychological intervention has diversified into several professions. Whereas in the past one person might be expected to bear the sole responsibility for helping a child, there now exist several resources that can be relied on. Specialists in speech, occupational, and physical therapy can assist with specific issues, while reading, writing, and math specialists can target weaknesses in academics. Counselors and psychologists help with emotional functioning, while medical doctors monitor physical health. Neuropsychologists are somewhat unique in that we typically look at the entire picture during assessment – by assessing cognition, health, and psychological functioning within the context of the child's environment, we can develop specific intervention plans uniquely suited for your family. One of the most important settings that neuropsychologists are involved with is your child's school.

Public School System

The development of special education services within the public school system rose out of a need to provide access for children with disabilities. The initial attempts to develop standardized assessment methods were historically rocky (see footnote 1) although the current system has improved since then. This system is designed to accommodate both the enormous increase of public schools and the students within them that need special accommodations. As with many large-scale programs, there remain individuals who "slip through the cracks," but if you understand how the system works then it can be better navigated.

The current model was born out of the Individuals with Disabilities Education Improvement Act (IDEA, 2004) in which the United States government recognized that the IQ/achievement discrepancy was problematic in identifying children with learning disabilities. With this model discarded, new methods of identifying learning disabilities had to be developed. Many educators began to use a set of procedures called Response To Intervention (RTI). RTI models rely on periodic curriculum-based standardized assessments to identify children who are at risk for low academic achievement. First teachers monitor the children and those who seem to struggle. Those who are behind are moved to a smaller environment where a teacher or learning specialist works more closely with the child. Children who still do not show satisfactory progress are then referred for special education services. At each stage, frequent and brief assessments are administered to gauge a child's progress.

It should be noted that federal and state legislation can vary, and the way that a specific school interprets these legislations can also vary. In general, however, IDEA specifies thirteen eligibility categories for special education (see footnote 2). An Individualized Education Program (IEP) committee must identify whether a student is eligible for special education due to one of these categories, and then determine which accommodations will be provided for the student. The specific accommodations recommended often are borne out from a psychoeducational or neuropsychological evaluation. These accommodations are placed in the IEP, which outlines the specific goals and interventions that will be used to help an individual child based on his or her needs. Each IEP has a team consisting of parents, the student, a case manager, a general educator, and a school psychologist. Additional members of the team may include neuropsychologists, other psychologists, tutors, advocates, social workers, and other therapists, i.e. speech and occupational therapy. The IEP team meets at least every year (and as often as parents require) to track progress, and modifications to the plan may be made based on results. In addition, the child must undergo a reevaluation every three years to determine if services need to be altered.

Another law is Section 504 of the Rehabilitation Act, which is intended to stop discrimination against people with disabilities. 504 plans consider children with any disability and is thus broader than an IEP; if your child doesn't qualify for an IEP he or she may qualify for a 504 plan. 504 plans are similarly aimed to provide tailored accommodations designed to optimize a child's learning. The 504 team is smaller than the IEP team and may just include parents and teachers. In addition, outside evaluations are not required; while parents can certainly seek outside consultation, a 504 plan is usually contained within the school itself.

Both IEPs and 504s are free services that all public schools, including charter schools, offer. They can often be instrumental in tailoring a specific program to suit your child's needs. There are some issues to note, however. As these laws are institutionalized at the federal level, the specifics that pertain to your child may not always apply. For example, IDEA mandates that an IEP must be "reasonably designed" in allowing children access to educational benefits. The fact that this wording focuses on a non-specific term allows for subjectivity in what is "reasonable." Furthermore, children must simply be allowed access; whether they actually benefit from whatever is accessible is not part of the law. Therefore, an IEP plan may be implemented but the services it offers might not actually benefit your child.

If you are unsatisfied with your child's progress under an IEP/504 plan, there are ways you can resolve your disputes. One common dispute is that a public school won't respond to a request from the parents. The reasons for a lack of response vary but often relate to limited resources and time. However, the law stipulates that the school must meet your child's needs and so continued advocacy for your child is a critical part of the process. As a first step, you can always ask for another IEP meeting to reconvene to address any issues that need to be resolved. You have the right to file a due process hearing and schools will often come to a resolution with you. In fact, one advocate I spoke with informed me that approximately 95% of hearings are ultimately resolved in a satisfactory manner for parents.

I urge parents to record letters, emails, and all documentation related to the IEP in case there is an upcoming dispute. You always have the right to file a complaint. If you take steps down this avenue I encourage you to contact a special education attorney. In fact, one advocate I spoke with informed me that approximately 95% of hearings are ultimately resolved in a satisfactory manner for parents. Such advocates are specifically trained to assist parents in securing the appropriate services for their children.

I'd like to end this section on a positive note, such that IEPs and 504s are ultimately designed to serve families with children who have special needs. Most people on an IEP/504 team are there because they are invested in your child's education and growth – there are times where outside intervention is needed, but for many families, these federal programs provide an invaluable service within the public school system.

Private Schools

Private/independent schools pose their own unique considerations. Private schools are not required to follow IEPs (see footnote 3) – however, many are very much interested in what an evaluation has to say and will take steps to modify their curriculum accordingly. As one private educator told me, a real positive impact can take place when there is an effective mix of "policy and people." Policy is the policy within the private school itself, which often resembles the models set forth by IDEA and Section 504 such that a service plan is provided with explicit goals and accommodations set in place. When a service plan is in place, parents and educators can openly communicate about the child in question. This ties in with the people; when all involved trust that they are working in tandem for the child, then open communication and collaboration will occur.

It is always important to understand the culture of your child's private school. Such schools will have their own approach towards handling evaluations and cognitive/learning issues and knowing about this approach in advance can alleviate any concerns or fears about an evaluation. There are also private schools are specifically designed for children with learning issues and have school psychologists and special educators who are well acquainted with evaluations.

Implementation of Accommodations

Whether public or private, I find that the greatest effect shows when there is coordinated care among all the adults responsible for the child's education. The neuropsychologist can connect families to the correct resources specific to the child's needs.

When part of an IEP/504 team, we often collaborate with the school psychologist in integrating our findings directly for the school. In private schools we serve similar roles, although sometimes we directly work with the families and teachers if a special educator is not available. The recommendations for accommodations we make vary considerably from case to case. The following table has examples of some of the more frequent accommodations that schools can implement.

Recommendation	Sample Reasons for Recommendation	Example
Preferential seating	Attentional/executive issues, hyperactivity, social and sensory issues	Jim has trouble focusing in class, and so the teacher has him sit up front and away from distractions.
Separate testing environment	Attentional/executive issues, hyperactivity, social and sensory issues, test anxiety, learning disabilities	Mercy's reading disability particularly emerges during tests, so she is allowed to go to smaller, private room and takes tests with a proctor to avoid distraction.
Smaller classrooms	Attentional/executive issues, hyperactivity, social and sensory issues, learning disabilities	The school has a second reading class of only 4–5 children where those with learning issues can have more direct interaction with teachers.
Extended time/ Testing over multiple sessions	Attentional/executive issues, slowed processing speed, learning disabilities, test anxiety	Mike is allowed time and a half on all reading tests, which he takes separately from the other children.
Grading modification	Learning disabilities, slowed processing speed	In recognition of her math disability Jenny is graded for setting up a math problem correctly, rather than getting the actual problem correct.
Token economy system	Attentional/executive and behavioral issues, impulsivity	Ms. Jones sets up a chart with stickers that reward for good behavior – enough stickers can extend to bonuses such as extra recess or less homework.
Additional classroom management strategies	Attentional/executive and behavioral issues, impulsivity, social and sensory issues	Mr. Rylin begins each day reviewing the classroom rules. He incorporates a timer during tests with 30 and15 minute warnings to keep students on task. He has a chart with daily, weekly, and monthly goals for the class.

Recommendation	Sample Reasons for Recommendation	Example
Audio recordings	Attentional/executive issues, receptive language problems, reading disabilities	Tim is allowed to use his smart phone to tape his Biology class, so he can revisit concepts later in the privacy of his home.
Word processor	Disorder of written expression, expressive language disorder, slowed processing speed	Chandra is allowed to work on a laptop in writing class to more effectively communicate her ideas.
Graphing paper/ calculator	Math disabilities, developmental coordination disabilities	Alexander is provided a specialized graph paper during math class to help him line up his numbers properly. He is allowed to use a special graphing calculator during the midterm.
Organizational planner	Attentional/executive issues	Students in Mr. Ho's class receive a specialized planner that provides a calendar, homework section, and other guides to assist with management.
On-campus tutoring services	Learning disabilities	Ms. McGrath is the on-campus reading specialist. Children with diagnosed reading disabilities are allowed to spend a portion of their homeroom class with her instead.
Integrated education	Learning disabilities emotional, and behavioral problems	The teachers and parents decide to pick a common theme each month to help Liatt with her studies. One month the class focuses on learning about cities, and in response to this Liatt's parents take her downtown to visit City Hall. Another month the theme is the ocean, and so they take a trip to the aquarium.

This list is by no means exhaustive. Speak with your school and your neuropsychologist about how your child's specific needs might best be met. I encourage all parties to be creative; often there are ways to address a child's problems in a specific way that highlights his or her individuality (see footnote 4).

Other Professionals

There are many other members of the child's treatment team. Before I detail these, parents might be concerned about the cost of these services. It is true that services can add up so, it is important to decide which, if any of these are appropriate for your child. Many local regional centers and hospitals provide some of these services for free or at a discount, or may take insurance.

Speech & Language Therapists: Speech therapists are the go-to professionals for expressive and receptive language issues. They can also often assist with reading disabilities. Speech therapists address all manner of issues related to speech; they can teach phonics, target speech impediments such as lisps and slurred words, improve receptive language skills, and teach grammar, syntax, and spelling. Speech therapists can also improve social communication skills and assist children in interacting more effectively with peers and adults.

Occupational Therapists: Occupational therapists target fine and gross motor issues. Children who struggle with coordination, handwriting, typing, and those with hand injuries can benefit from OT. These therapists also provide therapy for children with sensory regulation issues.

Physical Therapists: Physical therapists, like occupational therapists, assist children with motor delays and injuries. Children who are recovering from injury or illness, or those with coordination issues often are referred for PT.

Educational Specialists: Educational specialists focus on a child's academic development. Some specialists focus on a specific area such as reading or math while others are broader in scope. There is a considerable range of professionals who provide supplemental education, from tutors to professionals with doctoral degrees who use specific techniques to help your child learn.

Behavioral Specialists: A behaviorist assists in designing a structured system for you and your child by identifying stressors in the environment that lead to undesirable behaviors. Such services can be helpful when your child is disruptive within the environment and/ or when he or she requires additional structure. Behaviorists will come up with a functional behavior assessment, which breaks down problem behaviors in the child and comes up with interventions designed to address the problem behaviors. This assessment looks at why a behavior occurs and considers social, emotional, cognitive, and environmental influences, going beyond the "what" of problem behaviors and endeavoring to answer the "why" and "how".

A subset of behavioral specialists works with children on the autistic spectrum. State funding may be available to assist your family financially in securing an appropriate resource.

Substance Counselors: Children and adolescents with substance use issues are often referred to treatment centers. Some centers are inpatient while others are intensive outpatient groups. Depending on the nature and severity of the issue, a substance use counselor may also see patients on a weekly basis..

Psychologists/Mental Health Specialists: Psychotherapy is a common referral when an emotional component is in play. Chapters 1 and 6 cover these in more detail.

Medical Professionals: Primary physicians, neurologists, and psychiatrists often work with neuropsychologists in coordinating a child's physical and mental care. Chapter 1 provides additional detail.

This chapter examined the role that neuropsychologists play within the school system, and reviewed other professionals who may be of assistance for you and your child. I close by emphasizing that coordination of care is the key for implementation of care. First and foremost, be sure you work with professionals whom you trust, who are available, and who are willing to share information not just with you, but with each other in the sole interest of helping your child thrive.

FOOTNOTE 1

Early IQ tests were quite biased towards Caucasian individuals and so a disproportionate number of minorities were segregated into special education classes. The *Larry P. vs. Riles* case directly addressed this by noting that IQ tests that were standardized on white, upper-middle class children were being used on African American children from a lower socio-economic background to diagnose mental retardation. Since this ruling, IQ tests cannot be used as the main determinant in identifying a child with special needs.

FOOTNOTE 2

The thirteen disabilities covered by IDEA are: autism, deaf-blindness, deafness, emotional disturbance, hearing impairment, intellectual disability, multiple disabilities, orthopedic impairment, other health impairment, specific learning disability, speech/language impairment, traumatic brain injury, and visual impairment. Of note, ADHD isn't explicitly listed as one of the disabilities although sometimes it is subsumed under "other health impairment." 504 plans are another way to seek accommodations for ADHD.

FOOTNOTE 3

Although private schools are not required to follow IEPs, many will still be open to tailoring a curriculum to meet similar standards. Furthermore, children who attend a private school specifically because of a learning issue will be eligible for the modifications outlined in the IEP. Private schools will accommodate 504 plans if they receive any federal funding, as Section 504 applies to all recipients of such funds.

FOOTNOTE 4

In a personal anecdote, one boy who struggled with attentional problems during reading class behaved much better once he was assigned the crucial role of "Reading Monitor." As the monitor, it was his responsibility to set up the carpet for storytime five minutes before the teacher started reading. He also had a notebook where he had to identify the main characters and their conflict. This boy, who loved to be the center of attention, was then tasked to ask *other* kids about the story. He took to this responsibility quite well and made sure to think of difficult questions in an attempt to stump his classmates!

PART II

COMMON DIAGNOSES AND SYNDROMES

CHAPTER 9

Specific Learning Disorders

Children often struggle in one or more areas of reading, mathematics, and writing. When these struggles are significant enough to pose a consistent hindrance to school achievement, a specific learning disorder might be involved.

Specific learning disorders (SLDs) are a group of conditions that characterize children who have difficulties in one of seven academic areas including listening comprehension, expressive language, basic reading skills, reading comprehension, written language, mathematical calculation, or mathematical reasoning. Children often struggle in more than one of these areas even when they have high intellectual abilities. As you may have seen with your child, learning disorders can lead to stress and anxiety for children, who often perceive that they are struggling more than their peers. This can lead to emotional and behavioral issues down the line. Fortunately, interventions for learning disorders can result in remarkable progress, although some children will always struggle depending on the severity of the disorder.

If you are reading this chapter, perhaps you have a child who has a diagnosed or suspected learning disorder. You might worry that a learning disorder reflects something about your child's overall abilities, or that it will be a significant handicap for your child's ability to succeed in life. Parents often experience frustration, guilt or confusion after discovering their child has a learning disorder.

Rest assured that a learning disorder does not speak to your child as a whole. He or she might have a weakness in a certain area, but this is not reflective of their intellectual abilities. This can be a way to explain the results to your child – you can highlight how smart they are, but also show understanding as to why they don't always feel so smart. We all have strengths and weaknesses, and sometimes those weaknesses translate towards school achievement. Sometimes, your child might have weaknesses in more than one area – however, we can usually find an explanation for why there are multiple struggles. Below I offer a few metaphors that can sum up some of the experiences of having a learning disorder. These can be used both for your own understanding and in explaining what is going on to your child.

The Incredible Machine (for a single SLD): The brain is a complex machine that performs most of its functions without our even being aware of it. When we go for a swim, or talk to a friend, we do it without giving it a second thought. However, like all machines there are innumerable little parts that make up your brain. Sometimes, if a single part is not working to its peak efficiency, the whole machine feels like it is struggling a bit, even if the rest is working smoothly. That's what's going on with a learning issue – the rest of the brain is working just fine, but you notice that one issue all the more because it is the one part that is *not* working to its best!

The Overworked Boss (for more than one SLD): Think of the brain like a CEO of a company. It has to keep a number of different functions going – some can never be turned off, like breathing and heart rate. Others are more active during specified tasks, like reading and writing, or during specified times, like dreaming. All bosses have some workers who work better than others. When a few workers are less efficient, the boss has to focus on them more. This comes at the expense of running the whole company properly. Therefore, when more than a few workers are not working to their best, this boss-brain can become overworked and run the whole company less efficiently. In the same way, when children have more than one learning difficulty they might fatigue quicker or feel like their brain is working too slowly.

Riding a Bicycle (for SLDs when there is trouble with automaticity): Think back to the first time you rode a bike. Wasn't it difficult? You had to focus on balancing on the seat, arranging your feet on the pedals, navigating the handle bars, and making sure the whole thing didn't tip over! Then, after some time it all became natural and you stopped having to think about what you were doing. Just like bike riding, reading/writing/math require multiple steps to do well. When looking at others who have mastered these steps, it looks like a single, cohesive element. However, for some people it just takes longer to get there - they still have to think of all the elements required to properly read/write/solve math problems. This struggle can slow them down and make the work seem much more intensive — this is what a lack of automaticity means.

Cause

We do not yet fully understand the cause of SLDs. Learning disorders have shown correlative evidence with neuroimaging studies (see footnote 1) and they do run in families. In line with this, there is genetic evidence for SLDs (see footnote 2). However, SLDs are principally diagnosed based on how a child is functioning in his or her academic environment.

Some children may simply develop more slowly than other children. In mild cases of SLD, the learning disorder may have emerged because the child was initially in the low average range of an academic ability. However, because the academic curriculum compounds over time, this low average ability eventually leads to additional delays. Milder SLDs may also be more prominent in academically enriched environments, where children are expected to achieve at a higher-than-average level. In such an environment, a child who may never have been detected at a more typical school might show signs of struggling.

Reading Disorders

When a child has significant and consistent issues with reading, a reading disorder might be the explanation. Reading involves a complex synchronization of several cognitive and sensory processes. Neuropsychologists usually examine both silent (receptive) reading and oral (expressive) reading skills. Children who struggle with either might do so because they have difficulties with phonics, phonological processing, fluency, and/or comprehension.

> *The results of Andrew's evaluation were in. The neuropsychologist highlighted that Andrew's verbal intelligence was exceptional, with a score that put him at the 95th percentile. This surprised his parents, who were seeking answers for his long struggles with reading. However, they soon learned that his reading struggles were due to a generally slowed processing speed, and a delay in processing the sounds of words. Andrew's weakness in auditory processing in turn interfered with his ability to learn phonics and as such, he was not confident while reading aloud. Over time, Andrew began to compensate for his struggles by "guessing" at words, often saying the completely wrong word while reading. This hit close to home with his parents, who were stumped how their normally careful and conscientious son seemed to adopt an almost haphazard, random approach to his reading.*

Phonics refers to the way written parts of words are sounded out. Children who have delays in their phonics will experience increased difficulty in reading as the material becomes more advanced in later grades. Phonological processing refers to a child's ability to hear how words are properly pronounced and often go hand-in-hand with phonics, although sometimes children perform better in one area over the other. Fluency refers to how quickly and smoothly someone can read the material while comprehension taps into one's ability to understand what he or she has read. One advantage of the neuropsychological evaluation is the ability to examine some of the underlying sensory and cognitive processes that might affect these various aspects of reading (see footnote 3).

Dyslexia is a term used to describe some children with reading disorders. As mentioned in Chapter 4, not all children with a reading disorder might meet the classic "dyslexic" pattern, which is usually characterized by confusion with phonics and phonemes in general, along with associated impaired fluency. For example, a child might be able to read fluently and pronounce most words correctly but struggle with comprehension, which may be related more to general verbal reasoning or attention rather than classic dyslexia. However, some educators and practitioners will use this term to refer to any sort of reading disorder.

Mathematics Disorders

Children with a disorder in mathematical abilities struggle in one or more fundamentals of math, which include basic calculation skills, general mathematical knowledge and reasoning, and visual-spatial thinking. Some children may excel in one of these areas only to find themselves struggling when a new concept is introduced, such as algebra or geometry. Working memory and executive functioning often explain some of the struggles with mathematical ability. Children who favor concrete thinking styles may struggle more with the more abstract aspects of some concepts. Some children find the "big picture" aspects of word problems more appealing than the detail-oriented work required for calculation.

Victoria's calculation skills were actually found to be quite strong, which was a bit of a surprise given her poor math grades last year. Her neuropsychologist went on to explain that she had achieved automaticity in calculating basic arithmetic problems but would sometimes make careless errors that lowered her score on tests. More importantly, her haphazard approach to problems really affected her ability to solve multi-step problems; she would focus on each individual part without seeing the "big picture" of how to properly set an equation up. In addition, Victoria had some mild attentional issues which made it difficult for her to read through longer word problems – this was found to simultaneously affect her reading and her math achievement.

In Victoria's case, at least some of her difficulties in mathematics can be attributed to problems with attention and focus, which can interfere with her ability to comprehend word problems and properly set up equations. Other children might primarily struggle in processing the individual numbers and signs, resulting in computation errors (see footnote 4). Still other children might have trouble retrieving previously learned math facts and applying them to new problems, which may reflect a more general difficulty with long-term memory retrieval.

Disorders of Written Expression

Roger is a brilliant young boy who can give a rousing speech in front of his class and friends, reads books two grade levels above his expected level, and aces his mathematical tests. However, he absolutely dislikes writing. Teachers are perplexed by Roger's written work, which often consists of a single sentence or two. When prompted, he will simply say, "That's all I can think of" or "Nothing else comes to mind." This is in sharp contrast to his oral expression abilities. Roger undergoes testing and results reveal that his spelling is fine, but Roger struggles in organizing his thoughts when transcribing them on paper. Furthermore, he demonstrated some mild fine motor delays that made writing in general an effortful and frustrating processing.

Written expression impairments account for a smaller percentage of SLDs but nonetheless may emerge, either in concert with another disorder or in isolation. Many children with reading disorders also have problems with writing if they struggle with processing written material in general. Difficulties with phonics often are evident with spelling errors, while fine motor problems can interfere with the physical aspects of writing. Other times, the source of the problem lies in expressive language abilities which simultaneously make speaking and writing a challenge. In Roger's case, his weakness appears linked in part to executive difficulties in planning and organizing exactly what he wants to write.

Treatments and Implications

There now are multiple interventions available for SLDs. Rarely, however, will you find a single "cure-all" that will quickly and efficiently fix the issues. Rather, special educational services, some which are offered at the schools themselves, can help your child with their delays. One common theme among all SLDs is that the earlier interventions are put into place, the better the outcomes. This is in part because academic work grows exponentially over the years, and so children have "further to fall behind" if they continuously struggle, and also partially due to motivational issues. A six-year-old may still have a love for reading despite experiencing difficulties, but that same love might diminish during adolescence if the struggles continue without aid.

For reading, programs generally focus on teaching phonics, orthographics (the ability to recognize the visual pattern of letters), and vocabulary, associating words with images or their sounds, and learning to "visualize" scenes while reading full sentences.

Mathematics can be taught using visual cues (e.g. physical objects in place of numbers) and using self-monitoring strategies to assist with setting up and solving problems correctly. For writing, interventions can target spelling, handwriting, or written expression using methods developed by occupational therapists and educational specialists. Sometimes, a speech therapist might assist with any of the above issues if an expressive or receptive language component is identified.

Recently, there has been increased interest in using web-based instruction to assist. There now are several applications that are designed to assist in learning skills relevant to the learning disorder in question. In general, it is best to use these only as a supplement to curriculum provided by an educational specialist.

With intervention, I have seen many children make remarkable progress in their learning issues. Sometimes, a learning disorder can even be "outgrown" as a child ages, although this is more common with milder SLDs. In cases where the child has more difficulty, intervention can ameliorate some of the delays, but accommodations must also be considered. Such accommodations can be implemented by schools – either through an IEP/504 plan or under the policy of the independent school. Chapter 8 reviews some possible accommodations that may be suitable for your child.

FOOTNOTE 1

There is evidence for structural and functional differences in several parts of the brain that are linked to SLDs. Reading and writing disorders seem to be linked to areas involved in phonological processing and visual systems, while mathematical disorders have been associated with the parietal regions, which are implicated in visual spatial processing. Dysfunction in the frontal lobes have also been associated with SLDs.

FOOTNOTE 2

Studies have long searched for a genetic basis for SLDs, in part because there is increased prevalence among family members and particularly among twins. The concordance rate for identical twins and reading disorders are estimated to be approximately 50%, which suggests that both environmental and genetic factors are at play. There may be evidence that certain aspects of reading are more genetic in nature, while others are more influenced by the environment, although research on this is still emerging.

FOOTNOTE 3

Briefly, here are some of the domains that may explain why your child struggles in certain aspects of reading. Phonics are linked to expressive language and visual processing, the latter of which relates to orthographics, or the ability to recognize the patterns of letters. Phonological processing is linked to receptive language, attention/working memory, and auditory processing. Fluency is linked to visual processing, sustained attention, and processing speed. Comprehension is also associated with visual processing, as well as attention, verbal intelligence/vocabulary, and executive abilities. Sometimes multiple areas are affected and have downstream impacts on more than one area of reading; other times, children may have found a way to compensate for some delays using their own strategies that does not assist with other issues (e.g. learning to "guess" a word after sounding out the first parts of it).

FOOTNOTE 4

Sometimes, a reading disorder blends into a mathematics disorder when orthographic processing is delayed. Children who have trouble recognizing the letters may experience similar struggles with numbers and signs. As such, dyslexia may often emerge through computation errors (switching signs or reversing numbers). A reading disorder might also impact a child's ability to comprehend word problems. This highlights that few SLDs are cleanly isolated; disruption in one area can impact multiple subjects because of the overlap in their cognitive demands.

CHAPTER 10

Other Learning Disorders

The specific learning disorders account for reading, mathematics, and writing difficulties. However, children may exhibit neurodevelopmental delays in other areas including language, coordination, sensory processing, and nonverbal body language. This chapter reviews the disorders that may explain these delays.

The SLD triad of reading, mathematics, and writing are primarily concerned with delays in one or more of these areas in terms of academic achievement. However, children may experience delays in other cognitive and motor functions, which may indirectly affect a core academic area, and even be the underlying cause of a SLD. Other times they stand somewhat separately and yet still interfere with a child's day-to-day life.

Receptive and Expressive Language Disorders

Michael is a nine-year-old boy in the third grade. His teachers have expressed some concerns that Michael doesn't seem to be able to attend to the material in class. He will often sit quietly and appear lost during teacher instruction. Recently, one teacher highlighted an incident in which she asked Michael to put away the toys after an activity. Michael picked up some toys and then stood by the cubbyholes where the toys go with a confused look on his face. It was only after multiple promptings that Michael was able to put away the toys. Teachers also note that he is quiet, rarely participates in class, and has trouble with reading. They suggest that Michael undergo testing to determine whether he has an attentional disorder.

Does Michael qualify for ADHD? Perhaps – another possible explanation is that he has a mixed expressive-receptive language disorder. Children who struggle in speech and language may have some neurodevelopmental delays in language acquisition. There is neuroanatomical evidence that such children might have changes in their brains that directly link to the language processes (see footnote 1). Such children might also have struggles in attention and processing speed which interfere with their ability to acquire language. Language disorder often accounts for struggles in reading and written expression; oftentimes a child who struggles in oral reading and writing will have an expressive language disorder which accounts for both conditions.

The language system is complex and one modality (e.g. writing) might be preserved while another one is affected (e.g. speaking). A distinction must also be made between expressive and receptive language abilities. Children with an expressive language disorder may struggle with naming, verbal memory, grammar, and semantics (i.e. word meaning). Such children might struggle speaking and/or writing in complete sentences, and may report a paucity of thought content by saying something like "nothing comes to my mind."

In the case of a receptive language disorder, children do not just have trouble expressing themselves but struggle in comprehending what others say to them. As children generally need to be able to understand others before speaking clearly themselves, it would be unusual to see a child with *only* a receptive language disorder – usually, both expressive and receptive systems are impacted (see footnote 2). Such children may appear inattentive when in truth they do not comprehend what they are hearing. They may struggle with more complex sentences and appear confused when given verbal instructions.

A comprehensive assessment can pinpoint exactly where the language delay occurs. Children might have delays in understanding phonics or syntax, which can lead to simplified sentences and mispronounced words. Other children might struggle putting thoughts or ideas into words, or speaking fluently. Another aspect of language is that of social pragmatics, or the subtle mechanisms required for successful social conversation. Difficulties in this area are often observed in children who are on the autistic spectrum.

Speech therapists are trained clinicians who know how to assess and treat speech and language disorders. They can address issues with phonics, articulation, fluency, comprehension, and pragmatics and some specialize in motoric deficits that might contribute to any language delays. Therapists will teach your child vocabulary, practice conversation, and teach strategies to overcome cognitive issues that might be affecting your child's language abilities (e.g. slowed processing speed). There is quite a bit of research on the effectiveness of speech therapy and you can rest assured that a competent therapist will be of great service to your child if he or she has a language disorder.

Developmental Coordination Disorder

When motor coordination interferes with your child's functioning, a developmental coordination disorder (DCD) might be involved. While on occasion it is a sole diagnosis, DCD often is secondary to other conditions including ADHD, language disorders, autistic spectrum disorders, or neurological injury (see footnote 3).

Motor functions are roughly split into "fine" and "gross" motor skills. Fine motor skills relate to movements that primarily involve hand-eye coordination. Tying shoes, writing, holding a fork, and typing all require fine motor movements. Gross motor skills relate to movements that involve the whole body, like running, swimming, and whole-body coordination required to play sports. Children might develop one area well while experiencing delays in the other. Delays in either can lead to academic and social difficulties. Children might feel inadequate while playing sports, or gain weight because of general inactivity. They might appear "clumsy" or "slow" to their peers. Given that a DCD is often present in any number of other conditions, it may further complicate an attentional, learning, or social issue.

While children sometimes can outgrow some of their motor difficulties as they age, many will continue to experience issues with coordination later in life. Therefore, physical or occupational therapy, or a combination of both are the main recommendations when a DCD is diagnosed. Physical therapists are often called upon either when there is a clear injury of the body, or when gross motor functions are the primary area of concern. In contrast, occupational therapists are often used to assist with fine motor skills, and tend to tie motor movements directly with the functional needs of the child.

Occupational therapy can either focus on bottom–up techniques such as sensory stimulation, kinesthetic training, and perceptual-motor training (see footnote 4) or top–down methods that focus on using one's mind and body to learn specific skills and solve specific problems. The bottom–up approach trains a child in areas they might be lacking (e.g. practicing fine motor control of the wrist using a standardized measure to track changes) while a top–down approach takes into account a child's desires in treatment (problem-solving how to successfully kick a soccer goal). Some therapists prefer one strategy over another and I encourage you to discuss the pros and cons of each with the therapist, should a need for occupational therapy arise.

Sensory Processing Disorders

Disruptions in sensory information processing can have significant effects on a child. Sensory processing disorders were historically lumped into another diagnosis, such as a learning or language disorder or an autistic spectrum disorder, but recently there has been increased interest in independently evaluating for these conditions. Some practitioners will argue that disruptions in sensory processing and integration account for many of the symptoms seen in ADHD or an autistic spectrum disorder (see footnote 5). Therapists might target the senses as the initial point in intervention, with the idea that by resolving issues at this level, higher-order functions involving attention, memory, and executive functions will resolve. Broadly, most practitioners will examine both visual and auditory processing to establish whether disruption lay in either of these two modalities.

Jeanette is an easily distractible young girl who never fails to make a disturbance at home, school, or church. She was diagnosed early on with attention deficit/hyperactivity disorder and was undergoing pharmaceutical intervention to address her problems. Although the medication assisted with her impulsive behavior, she still had broad learning struggles in reading and writing. She later underwent a more comprehensive evaluation that revealed that Jeanette struggled in processing auditory information. While other children could more easily filter out noise, Jeanette took in all auditory information, which at times overwhelmed her. She would compensate for this by fidgeting and talking, which distracted her from the overstimulation. Her troubles with auditory processing also interfered with her development of vocabulary and phonics, which explained some of her academic struggles. Armed with this new knowledge, her parents and teachers were able to make more refined adjustments to help Jeanette with her school and home life.

When a child has difficulty with auditory processing, he or she might have trouble expressing themselves and scramble syllables and words while talking. They might struggle with following directions, or appear easily distractible. Such children may have poorer musical ability or have trouble following social pragmatics related to the tone and rate of conversation. This can have downstream effects on reading, spelling, and oral math problems. Some children experience sensory overload, as Jeanette did, and compensate for this through hyperactive behavior. Others engage in rituals or "tics" that help bring their level of arousal down. It is easy to see how many clinical diagnoses including an autistic spectrum disorder, SLDs, ADHD, and anxiety might in part stem from an auditory processing issue.

If an auditory processing disorder is suspected, a neuropsychologist often refers out to an audiologist for a more tailored assessment. Along with assessing hearing, audiologists will examine auditory discrimination, memory, and sequencing to assist in coming to a diagnosis. Treatments for an auditory processing disorder are often addressed when treating the general disorder that the child has; for example, speech therapy can simultaneously target expressive language issues while accounting for difficulties with auditory processing. Accommodations such as preferential seating, visually heavy tests, and assistive technology can also be leveraged.

Simply put, Bobby dislikes reading. Put him in front of a crowd and he'll orate a long and detailed speech about anything and everything. He solves math problems without much difficulty and loves to write long stories about pirates and dinosaurs. However, reading is hard for Bobby. He reads slowly and with effort, and within just a few minutes he will complain of headaches and fatigue. To his parents' surprise, the neuropsychologist suggests that some of Bobby's reading issues might be related to his vision. Upon recommendation, they take Bobby to an optometrist who confirms that Bobby struggles with visual convergence — in other words, his eyes have trouble converging in a smooth manner despite his 20/20 vision. Other things about Bobby suddenly make sense — such as his difficulty catching (but not throwing) a ball, a tendency to close one eye when reading, and general irritability and short attention span with reading.

Struggles with visual processing can be linked to mechanical issues, such as the convergence insufficiency described above, or relate to integration issues. As with an auditory processing disorder, visual processing disorders usually explain broader symptoms observed in learning (particularly reading) disorders, ADHD, and autistic spectrum disorder, among others. Children who struggle with integrating visual information with the rest of their senses might close their eyes, grow anxious or irritable, and generally become too distracted to focus on relevant material when they are visually overwhelmed. Visual processing disorders should be formally evaluated by an ophthalmologist or optometrist if the neuropsychologist detects a possible issue.

Treatments for visual processing disorders primarily are designed to accommodate and leverage a child's personal strengths. Some examples include using less visually distracting material, extra time for reading, and presenting material through oral/auditory modes. Some practitioners advocate for vision therapy, which is not without controversy (see footnote 6). When sensory integration is identified as a key issue, occupational therapy is an appropriate referral, as further described in Chapter 13. As with auditory processing disorders, often a treatment plan addresses the more general diagnosis with a few specific accommodations designed to address the sensory issues.

Nonverbal Learning Disorder

The concept of a NVLD emerged in the nineties and described children who exhibit struggles in visual and nonverbal abilities, which often translate into social-emotional and academic difficulties. Children with NVLD often struggle with hand-eye coordination, reading body language and social cues, and solving mathematical problems while exhibiting strengths in verbal reasoning and problem-solving. Such children also may experience anxiety in social situations and struggle with maintaining friendships and personal relationships. In many aspects, NVLD resembles a high functioning autistic spectrum disorder (i.e. Asperger's syndrome) and the differential diagnosis can be difficult to make (see footnote 7). Some practitioners might argue that there is no need for a distinction between the two as the treatments for both overlap. However, there are cases when a child might meet criteria for an autistic spectrum disorder with preserved nonverbal abilities, so in my viewpoint it is still worthwhile to consider these two diagnoses separately.

Treatments for NVLD include sensory-motor integration to help children grow more at ease with processing nonverbal information. Social skills training can assist with relationships, while cognitive strategies that include verbalizing visual information can assist with problem-solving and bolster visual skills. Children with NVLD often benefit from structure, explicit verbal guidelines, and controlled, nurturing environments that allow them to feel safe and able to focus on their growth in a relaxed manner.

FOOTNOTE 1

Research suggests that children with language disorders have anatomical differences in several brain regions. One key area of interest is the left-hemisphere auditory cortex, which is thought to be key in processing auditory information. Given that language is acquired primarily through auditory information, this structure may be implicated in some language disorders. Other risk factors of language disorders include cerebral volume and asymmetry, the cerebellum, and the parietotemporal cortex.

FOOTNOTE 2

A mixed-receptive expressive disorder is the official diagnosis for children who have trouble with both receptive and expressive language. Generally, this is considered a more severe language disorder as both comprehension and expression are affected. Children with a mixed receptive-expressive disorder are at an increased risk for learning disorders and emotional problems. Fortunately, speech therapy is an effective way to address these language delays.

FOOTNOTE 3

A developmental-coordination disorder is a "catch-all" term used to explain why children have motoric difficulties. The actual source of these difficulties can usually be identified, either based on a known neurological injury or because of a broader condition that affects the motor system along with other areas (e.g. autistic spectrum disorder). However, DCD is a stand-alone diagnosis and sometimes, there are children who are simply delayed in either their fine or gross motor systems. In this case, a sole diagnosis of DCD might be an appropriate way to capture the difficulties that these children experience.

FOOTNOTE 4

Sensory integration is a form of occupational therapy that focuses on helping children become more comfortable with physical sensations. Children might play with balls or other toys of different textures and sizes. Special equipment allows children to swing or spin or otherwise use their bodies in a safe environment. Later on children might be tasked to go through specialized obstacle courses or engage in other more physical activities. Kinesthetic training focuses on having a child engage in specific physical activities such as acting, charades, and dance with positive reinforcement such as praise and awards. These activities are hierarchically arranged and progressively more challenging. Perceptual-motor training focuses on tasks that require both motor and perpetual tasks (e.g. balance beam, kicking a ball). I recommend speaking to your occupational therapist with any questions about these therapies.

FOOTNOTE 5

I always caution parents that although a sensory processing disorder may explain some of your child's symptoms, they are unlikely to explain *all* of the symptoms. Therefore, it would be premature to ascribe a child's attentional and behavioral issues as an "auditory processing disorder" when ADHD might still be the best diagnosis. It is generally better to view sensory processing issues as underlying contributions to other diagnoses. Although accommodations designed to limit auditory overstimulation might, in this case, assist with managing symptoms, they are unlikely to "cure" ADHD.

FOOTNOTE 6

Vision therapy involves a series of vision exercises designed to strengthen visual skills. Many doctors will promote vision therapy as a viable way to improve visual processing. However, the link between vision therapy and learning disabilities has not been established. While visual issues might explain some aspects of a reading disability, research does not support that vision therapy will fix such a disability. However, there is some research to suggest that vision therapy can help with other problems, such as a visual convergence insufficiency.

FOOTNOTE 7

Some practitioners distinguish NVLD from an autistic spectrum disorder by the method of diagnoses. NVLD is primarily a neuropsychological diagnosis; it is made based on findings that support a preference for verbal over visual information. An autistic spectrum disorder is primarily diagnosed through the reports of others and through a comprehensive intake history. A neuropsychological evaluation can be important for children on the spectrum as it still provides a profile of cognitive and academic strengths and weaknesses. Often, children on the spectrum will also qualify for a NVLD based on their test scores, which further characterizes the manner in which they process information.

CHAPTER 11

Attention-Deficit/ Hyperactivity Disorder

Attention-deficit/hyperactivity disorder (ADHD) is a disorder of self-control. Children with ADHD often have problems with attention, impulse control, and hyperactivity that can contribute to academic, social, and emotional difficulties. This chapter will review the neuropsychology of ADHD.

Attention-deficit/hyperactivity disorder, or ADHD, is one of the most widely recognized learning disorders. The brains of children with ADHD function differently from the brains of other children. These differences in function manifest as the common behavioral traits of ADHD, such as difficulty with attention, impulse control, and hyperactivity. Children might appear distracted, sluggish, or overly hyperactive and seemingly unable to restrain their behavior. Parents and teachers are often frustrated with the child's inability to respond to redirection and at times blame might be mistakenly assigned, either to the adults for poor disciplinary management or to the child for being "dysfunctional."

Of course, most children are at times inattentive, impulsive, and hyperactive. What distinguishes those children from children with

ADHD is the severity of these symptoms. It may help to envision ADHD not as a discrete illness, but rather a cluster of behaviors we all share that in some happen to gravitate towards an extreme continuum. Homework or class, which is often boring for many children, becomes much more painful for children with ADHD. As a metaphor, consider the difference between washing the dishes and scrubbing the entire kitchen. For most of us, washing the dishes is an inconvenient but tolerable chore that we usually do and then move on. For most kids, homework is like washing the dishes. For a child with ADHD, however, the prospect of homework is as immense a task as scrubbing the whole kitchen, stove, fridge and all. It seems insurmountable and overwhelming and as a consequence, it is put off for as long as possible.

Children with ADHD are not inattentive all the time. Actually, there is some evidence that such children can *overly* focus on things that they find rewarding and fun. Many children can become engrossed in a video game for hours, but for a child with ADHD, this focus can be excessive, and at the expense of everything else. Evolutionary psychologists have developed some interesting theories about the hyperfocus associated with ADHD (see footnote 1). Sometimes, this hyperfocus can be channeled in a manner that can lead to great creativity and productivity. However, this focus does not generalize, and generalized focus on many different things is often necessary to succeed at school. This is where children with ADHD will often stumble.

Saul is a delightful eight-year old boy who was referred for an evaluation. Dr. Smith sat with the parents and listened to some of their concerns. Saul is the youngest of four children and unlike his siblings, has always been a bit of a troublemaker. Saul's father recalled how Saul used to tantrum up until he was six years old. His parents, who were always vigilant with their children, found themselves at a loss how to manage Saul, who responded poorly to redirection and discipline. Dr. Smith then met with Saul, who was excited and eager to talk about his dogs and his video games. Saul was observed to wander around the room during testing and had to repeatedly be asked to sit back on the couch. On the neuropsychological tests, he performed very well on IQ and brief attention measures, but struggled on other tests that required him to inhibit himself, plan ahead over a multi-step problem, and sustain his attention on a computer task for twenty minutes. Of note, Saul at times seemed confused as to why he kept jumping ahead and impulsively responding to questions. He knew something was off but was unable to rein himself him. Dr. Smith later followed up with teachers and observed Saul at school. By the end of the evaluation, he was able to conclude that Saul met the criteria for ADHD.

As mentioned, ADHD is a disorder of self-control. Self-control is a developmental process – obviously a ten-year old is expected to have more self-control than a five-year old. But what of the ten-year old who does not? This lack of self-control is not due to any willful resistance. Think of our executive functions like a personal assistant for our brain – managing our schedules, remembering appointments, and holding other details that help us through the day. The struggle for children with ADHD is that their personal assistants are malfunctioning. In other words, their inattention and behavioral problems are not intentional in nature.

This is crucial to know, as many understandably frustrated parents and teachers will try traditional methods of disciplining a child with ADHD. When such methods fail, they may ascribe blame to the child and up the ante, as it were, in order to try to coerce the child to behave. However, children with ADHD struggle with regulating their behavior even in the face of consequences. They may internalize what adults and their peers say about them, that they are "disruptive" or "a class clown" or just plain "disobedient." This can lead to additional behavioral and emotional problems later on.

Children with ADHD are at an increased risk of depression, anxiety, substance use, and delinquent behavior later on in life. In order to reduce this risk, it is important that we are aware of how we respond to these children.

Cause

Much of our higher thought processes rely on the frontal lobes, or the large masses of brain matter that sit in the front of our skulls. At the very front of the frontal lobes lie the prefrontal cortex, a region of the brain necessary for concentration, impulse control, and emotional regulation. Deep within the brain are other regions collectively known as the basal ganglia. The basal ganglia are the source of specific brain neurons that operate on dopamine, a type of neurotransmitter (see footnote 2). For most of us, the basal ganglia send regular signals up through the frontal lobes (among other regions along the way) that allow us to use our prefrontal cortexes to the best of our abilities. This aids in inhibition, planning, and focusing our attention on important matters, a cluster of activities that fall under the spectrum of executive functioning. The prefrontal cortex is also implicated in *working memory,* a type of memory that relates to the conscious holding and manipulation of information for a specific purpose.

Sometimes, the basal ganglia, the frontal lobes, and other brain regions that rely on dopamine transmission are less efficient than what is typical in humans. This can result in less activity in the frontal lobes, which studies examining both electrical activity and blood flow in the frontal lobes have confirmed. This underactivity in turn leads to the difficulties often observed in children with the disability.

It is important to also know what does *not* cause ADHD. There is no evidence that ADHD can be triggered by diet, including excessive sugar. While sugar can make some children more active at times, it does not result in the prolonged attentional and activity changes observed in ADHD. Furthermore, systematic studies on sugar find that it has different effects on different children; some become more active as might be expected, but other children don't react at all while still others actually improve their behavior! Television, computers, video games, and SmartPhones are also frequently raised as a concern. While children with ADHD are often quite enmeshed in these activities, it is difficult to claim that any of these *cause* ADHD. Rather, these should be controlled and regulated (as they should be with all children), in part because children will engage with a screen at the expense of other activities.

Subtypes

Many times, the term "ADHD" is referred to as "ADD," which stands for attention-deficit disorder. There was a time when ADD was the principal diagnosis; however, the proper term now is always ADHD, perhaps in recognition of the frequent co-occurrence of hyperactive symptoms.

However, sometimes the term ADD is still used when the child has a subtype of ADHD that is primarily marked by inattention without the impulsive or hyperactive behaviors. The correct term for this diagnosis is ADHD-predominantly inattentive, while the more "classic" presentation is referred to as ADHD-combined. A third diagnosis, ADHD-predominantly hyperactive-impulsive, is sometimes offered, although usually children diagnosed with this subtype present similarly to those with the combined subtype. In contrast, the predominantly inattentive subtype presents quite differently, to the extent that some clinicians and scientists argue that it is distinct disorder.

David has never been a problem in class. In fact, one of his first grade teachers once commended how quietly he would sit through reading time. He was always described as a placid and well-behaved child up until third grade, when homework was introduced to the class. Suddenly, David was flagged for constantly forgetting his homework assignments. What was once praised as quiet and respectful was now criticized as "spacy." One teacher noted in his progress report that David liked to daydream and stare out the window. The same teacher expressed concern that he was always the last to turn in his math worksheets during class. Outside of school, David seems like a well-liked and popular boy among his peers.

David might have the inattentive subtype of ADHD. Such children often seem as if they are in a fog or otherwise sleeping and disengaged from what is going on around them. They may appear like an absent-minded professor, going from class to class with little awareness of what they are supposed to be doing. Often, they work slowly and demonstrate what might be called a sluggish cognitive tempo (see footnote 3). Of note, many with the inattentive type are undiagnosed, in part because such children rarely draw attention in the classroom.

Becca is a popular, well-liked fifth grader. She was just elected vice-president of the student council and was active on several committees. Parents and teachers were delighted by her outgoing, gregarious style. She loved to talk and sometimes this carried over into class, but her teachers indulged her and provided minimal correction. Becca was always on the go, whether at home setting up plans for the next day or at school, organizing and coordinating activities with her many friends. Her English teacher noted that Becca seemed to struggle with reading and suggested she undergo testing to see if she might be eligible for accommodations as she prepares for middle school next year. Her mother took her to see a psychologist, and was shocked to learn that Becca met criteria for ADHD-combined type.

Becca's case is not unusual. Not all children with ADHD exhibit the classic fidgety, overly hyperactive and disruptive presentation that is more easily detectable. Girls in particular may go undiagnosed as they often exhibit hyperactive symptoms differently from boys. They may present as very talkative and excitable, and those who are quite bright might simply appear driven and motivated. Unfortunately, ADHD is linked to real cognitive issues that can interfere with school. Boys and girls who are undiagnosed might feel that they are unable to keep up with their peers simply because they are not smart enough.

Neuropsychology of ADHD

ADHD can be diagnosed by any qualified physician or psychologist. The disorder is primarily diagnosed through a clinical interview, behavior rating scales, and collateral interviews with parents and teachers. Children who consistently exhibit symptoms of inattention, hyperactivity, and impulsivity, across multiple settings that emerged prior to the age of 12 might have ADHD. A diagnosis can only be conclusively made once other medical, emotional, and cognitive disorders are ruled out (see footnote 4).

A neuropsychological evaluation can assist in diagnosing any co-occurring learning disorders that emerged alongside ADHD. Many children with ADHD do qualify for a learning disorder, perhaps because their symptoms interfered with their academic progress or because a shared underlying weakness (e.g. working memory) contributes to ADHD and the learning disorder.

Along with identifying learning disorders, neuropsychologists can track cognitive weaknesses due to ADHD. The inattentive type often results in slowed processing speed – children aren't just slow because they are daydreaming, it actually takes more effort and exertion to perform work at a speed more developmentally appropriate. Children with the hyperactive/impulsive type often have trouble inhibiting behavior and organizing, planning, and initiating activity – difficulties in any of these can be detected with a comprehensive examination of executive functioning. Both subtypes often have weaknesses in working memory, and with such weaknesses comes an increased difficulty in learning new material. However, like all children, some have a natural preference for some types of material over others. Therefore, one child with ADHD might struggle in reading but be a gifted artist, while another can read and speak very well but lag behind in mathematics.

Sometimes a child diagnosed with ADHD actually has no academic issues at all – this particularly may occur when the child is very bright and attends a school that fits with his or her cognitive style. In such cases however, changes in setting may cause what were once subthreshold symptoms to emerge. Sometimes children breeze through elementary school only to struggle in high school, or even college, when there are increasing demands of organizational skills (i.e. executive functioning). Therefore, it is possible to be diagnosed with ADHD later in life, although usually at least some evidence of symptoms has been present for some time.

Treatments

The main treatments include behavior management, family therapy, and medication. In managing the behavior of your child, it is important to remember that children with ADHD have trouble with long-term prospects. While you can tell most nine-year olds to finish their homework before television, children with ADHD will have trouble tying homework (the immediate thing before them) to some far off reward (television at a later time). As such, feedback must always be immediate. Generally, frequent and positive feedback is best to help your child stay on task. Feedback that involves consequences and reprimand should be used sparingly if at all. This is because children with ADHD will often go off track or engage in an undesirable behavior. The research confirms that consequences, particularly ones that involve punishment, might work in the short-term but do little to enact long-term behavioral changes (see footnote 5).

Children with ADHD struggle with time management. They have little sense of an internal clock that will tell them how long things will take, and will act impatient and distractible as a result. To help mitigate this, consider using externalizing reminders of time to help your child stay on task. A timer, with a sign that says "you can do [insert desirable task] when the timer hits zero" will provide a concrete, external representation of what is required. In general, responsibilities and rewards should be made as tangible and present as possible. Don't be afraid to use reminders in the form of signs and cards, or implement a reward system with a visible progression such as a chart, to help maintain household rules in place.

Along with externalizing rules, guidelines, and rewards, consistency must always be used in carrying them out. This is an understandably difficult challenge for many parents, but its importance cannot be emphasized enough. All children are quite aware when rules aren't implemented consistently, and behavioral management strategies will inevitably fail. Try to maintain consistency across settings, and between partners to ensure that your child knows, understands, and can expect the system to work as planned.

Many children with ADHD are quite intelligent and some are exceptionally verbal. It can be therefore tempting to just try and reason with your child. However, conversation alone won't assist with change. Try to keep in mind that ADHD is a clinical disorder, and children with this condition process information in a manner that makes it hard for them to just "see reason" and act accordingly. However, always remember that this disorder is a challenge to deal with, and try not to put blame on yourself or your child when things go awry. Forgiveness of self and others is key in managing a child with ADHD.

Sometimes, the behavioral and academic problems are too much to cope with and you want to seek the help of a professional. There are many licensed therapists who may be suitable. For developing and implementing a behavioral management system, consider hiring the services of a board certified behavioral analyst (BCBA). BCBAs are consultants who will spend time with you, your family, teachers and your child across multiple settings. Through interviews, behavioral observations, and assessments, the BCBA can develop a plan that is tailored to help your child at home and school.

Other professionals are suitable when specific needs arise. Children and adolescents with ADHD often have social difficulties, and so social skills training may be warranted. Educational psychologists can assist with academic difficulties, though be sure the professional is familiar with teaching children with ADHD. Special educators may be available to help design and implement classroom management strategies. Individual psychotherapy may be warranted when emotional problems arise while family therapy is recommended when the struggles appear to be more systematic in nature.

Children and adolescents with ADHD are at an increased risk of conduct disorder. As described in Chapter 6, conduct disorder is a term used for youth with repeated delinquent and aggressive behavior towards others. Should signs of this emerge, a multi-systemic intervention is recommended.

Medication can be an effective method of controlling your child's symptoms, and there are times when it is highly recommended, at least on a trial basis. Most ADHD medications are stimulants that regulate dopamine in the brain, thus promoting frontal lobe functioning and the associated improvements in executive functioning. There is no scientific evidence that such medications harm the central nervous system or the brain. There is also little concern that a well-controlled medication regime will increase addictive behaviors; rather, children whose symptoms were controlled through adolescence are *less* likely to abuse illicit substances. There has been some discussion on the addictive properties of recreational stimulant use (see footnote 7).

Children who are medicated for ADHD will often exhibit marked improvements in their behavior. By improving attention and decreasing hyperactivity and impulsivity, such children will have better self-regulation and by extension, improved focus on their schoolwork. It is important to keep in mind that not all children respond to the medication and different types or doses may have been tried before an optimal "fit" is identified. As such, close and frequent contact with your pediatrician or child psychiatrist is essential. It may eventuate that medication is not the best option for your child – it certainly should not be assumed to be a "cure-all" that will fix everything. In my opinion, it is always a conversation to have when a child is diagnosed with ADHD, and I especially encourage parents to consult with a physician when their child's academics and emotional functioning are compromised.

There are side effects to consider, including decreased appetite, increased heart rate and blood pressure, and insomnia. A small but significant group of children may develop tics or anxious behaviors (e.g. skin picking) when taking stimulants – in such cases, medication can be adjusted or discontinued with no long-term effects. Regarding "permanent" effects of stimulant use, we certainly see that most children who are medicated have better academic, behavioral, and psychological short-term outcomes compared to those who go untreated, which bodes well for their long-term functioning. There is no evidence for long-term damage from stimulant use, although rigorous, long-term outcome studies of any drug are virtually impossible to carry out (see footnote 8). Therefore, it is most likely safe for your child to undergo a medication trial, and the benefits observed in successful cases generally outweigh any short-term side effects that may emerge.

Ultimately, the decision to medicate your child is yours to make. If you elect to try it, it is important that you find a physician whom you trust. Frequent contact is required, particularly early on as medication is first initiated and then adjusted. As stated, it is a safe option to use that can have great gains when your child's attentional difficulties are severe. Regardless of your decision, it is crucial to closely monitor your child's academic, behavioral, and psychological progress. While more challenging for them, this does not mean they will be unable to live happy and successful lives.

Life with ADHD

The García's are delighted to attend their son Luis' first day of college. There was a time when they thought he would never even finish high school, let alone enter college. In kindergarten his teachers noted that Luis was unable to socialize well with the other children. This extended into first grade, where during a parent-teacher conference his teacher said the dreaded words: "I think your son has ADD." They took Luis to see a doctor who made the diagnosis official. The family followed up with a school psychologist, who let them know that Luis was testing at pre-kindergarten levels in reading and spelling — along with ADHD, he was co-diagnosed with a reading disability. The family agreed to try putting Luis on a low-grade stimulant, but he didn't react well to it and seemed more irritable. They took him off medication and switched schools during second grade. He seemed to settle well here on his own, but then things started to fall apart in fourth grade. Luis was getting into fights at school and his reading continued to be way behind. The García's finally found a pediatrician who they liked and resumed medication. After some adjustments, he was able to graduate sixth grade. Middle and high school were rough for Luis, and he struggled keeping his grades up. In ninth grade, he got into a huge argument with a teacher and was suspended from school for two days. This prompted the García's to switch schools yet again. Tenth grade was much better — Luis started seeing a girl and was surrounded by better friends. His mood was much better and he demonstrated marked improvement in his focus and work. By twelfth grade, he managed a 3.2 GPA. His SATs were quite strong and he was admitted into a fairly competitive university nearby. Luis' parents knew that college would come with its own trials but felt that Luis was developing into a fine young man, one who was successfully learning how to manage his condition.

Stories like this are not at all unusual. There are many routes to take and no two paths are alike. In Luis' case, his family discontinued medication once before ultimately deciding it was the way to go. Even on medication, Luis' grades were poor and he was struggling with teachers. By tenth grade he had found the right mix of peers and environment that enabled him to thrive at school. His story highlights that the road is not straightforward. No child's road is, but ADHD does put more obstacles in the path. Successful navigation comes with help from the family and the greater community.

Most children with ADHD turn into adults with ADHD. In a few cases, people appear to "outgrow" the disorder, particularly as they age and their executive functioning system further matures. This is in part because adolescents and young adults are still developing their executive functions, which do not fully "peak" until the mid-twenties. For some adults with ADHD, they can successfully manage their symptoms on their own once they reach these peaks.

Other adults will continue to exhibit symptoms throughout their lives without treatment. Adults usually have diminished hyperactive and impulsive symptoms and generally experience difficulty with concentration and focus. Young adults may engage in more high-risk and sensation-seeking behaviors. Those who channel this positively might be very proactive and motivated. If an adult with ADHD finds their passion, then their proclivity to hyperfocus can be a great boon. For example, individuals with ADHD can work as successful engineers, computer programmers, entrepreneurs, and artists, among other careers that require drive and focus. Symptoms primarily arise when they are engaged in activities that do not interest them.

Risk comes when children with ADHD develop social and emotional struggles that persist into adulthood. Adults with depression and anxiety are more likely to engage in substance abuse and other risky behaviors. When an adult with ADHD has such struggles, the risk becomes quite high. Continued learning difficulties can limit college and future career aspirations. As such, early diagnosis and intervention is crucial. Once you understand why your child is struggling so much, you can start taking the steps to help your child succeed to the best of his or her abilities.

FOOTNOTE 1

ADHD has a strong genetic component, which has led scientists to hypothesize that it may have an evolutionary advantage that is no longer adaptable in our Western world. Until about ten thousand years ago, the majority of humans were nomadic hunter-gatherers. We had to constantly seek out food and shelter for the night and had to remain active, engaged, and ready to take on whatever challenges emerged as we foraged. It is not hard to see how someone with ADHD might thrive in such an environment. The "hyperfocus" we see now could be a leftover trait in which a subset of hunter/gatherers had to concentrate intently during key periods (e.g. while stalking an animal).

FOOTNOTE 2

Neurotransmitters are chemicals in the brain that influence neurotransmission, or the way neurons communicate with each other. Some neurotransmitters speed up this communication, while others slow it down. Still others interact with other chemicals in the brain to perform complex processes that ultimately influence neurotransmission even more. Dopamine is a specific type of neurotransmitter implicated in ADHD. We need dopamine to feel motivated, to experience pleasure, and to sustain focus over long periods of time. Many disorders are in part due to abnormal dopamine transmission, including ADHD, schizophrenia, and Parkinson's disease.

FOOTNOTE 3

A sluggish cognitive tempo sometimes is identified during evaluation. Children with a sluggish tempo are simply slower than average on measures of processing speed and automaticity. This is not due to motivational factors, but rather a fundamental inability to process information at an expected rate. As mentioned, a sluggish tempo is often a symptom of ADHD-predominantly inattentive type, although it can emerge in other disorders as well, such as those that follow brain injury.

FOOTNOTE 4

There are many other conditions that can mimic ADHD symptoms. These can range from the physical sources, such as low blood sugar, poor sleep, or a hearing problem, to psychological, such as depression or anxiety, or due to an autistic spectrum disorder, bipolar disorder, or a significant learning disorder. Therefore, ADHD should never be the "assumed" diagnosis if a child appears inattentive, hyperactive, or impulsive. Usually, a medical checkup combined with a psychological examination is sufficient to reach a diagnosis.

FOOTNOTE 5

Aversive consequences for undesirable behavior (e.g. "punishment") should generally be used sparingly with children with ADHD. Research shows that punishment can diminish behavior briefly but it also leads to resentment, avoidance, hostility, and subversive behavior. While the occasional aversive consequence might inform most children what their limits are, children with ADHD will be constantly testing these limits, often without being aware of this. Therefore, children with ADHD are going to be punished quite often, by other children or adults who do not know them. We know that increasing consequences at home is not effective. Therefore, praise, rewards, and teaching alternative behaviors (repeatedly at times) are always the strategies to use while managing a child with ADHD.

FOOTNOTE 6

Multi-systemic therapy is a type of therapy that involves the family and the community in addressing antisocial behaviors in youth. Therapists will work with the family, school, and community (e.g. sports teams, church, clubs) designed to help the child or adolescent engage in prosocial behavior. This type of therapy can be very involved and requires dedication from all parties involved, but it remains the most effective evidence-based method of treating conduct disorder.

FOOTNOTE 7

One myth about stimulants is that they only work when you have ADHD. The truth is, stimulants can make *anyone* feel more focused and attentive while they work. This has led some high school and college students to periodically use stimulants during exams. As such use is outside that of a doctor's prescription, it can lead to stimulant abuse and dependence. Constant use of stimulants outside of a safe dosage can lead to side effects such as insomnia, irritability, and withdrawal symptoms. Therefore, stimulants should only be used when closely monitored by a physician, and never as a temporary "fix" to help with schoolwork.

FOOTNOTE 8

The challenge with randomized, long-term studies is that such a study requires half of the participants (randomly assigned) to not take any medication. This is inherently unethical, as it limits treatment options. Current longitudinal studies can examine people who *voluntarily* took or did not take the treatment, but such studies are confounded by cohort effects. In other words, people who did take the medication will already have differences from those who did not, just by virtue of their choices. Random assignment is the only way to determine causality in a study and as mentioned here, it is often not ethically possible to set up such a design.

CHAPTER 12

Autistic Spectrum Disorders

The autistic spectrum disorders are characterized by impairment in social interactions and communication. Sometimes, verbal language, intelligence, and other aspects of cognition are affected as well. This chapter reviews the neuropsychology of these disorders.

Autistic spectrum disorders (ASD) are a group of neurodevelopmental disorders that share a profound deficit in social/communication skills. These disorders were once separately labeled under multiple names, including "autism," "childhood disintegrative disorder" and "Asperger's syndrome," among others, but recently all of these were merged under the single umbrella term of ASD. Although difficulties in social and communicative abilities remain the hallmark trait of children and adults on the spectrum, other abilities can widely vary in range. Children with ASD can range from the intellectually disabled up to the gifted with a broad range of ability in specific neurocognitive functions. Typically, ASD is diagnosed by a qualified psychologist or physician who has had experience working with this population. Sometimes a diagnosis can be made as early as two years of age, and symptoms of an ASD may emerge even earlier (see footnote 1). Children with higher functioning forms of ASD may not be detectable until after the age of two. An experienced neuropsychologist can certainly diagnose an ASD, although for older children, the neuropsychologist's role is perhaps best suited in identifying cognitive strengths and weaknesses of the child, along with co-occuring learning difficulties and emotional problems.

Etiology (Cause)

The etiology of ASD remains unclear. There is some evidence that perinatal complications can increase the risk of an ASD (see footnote 2). Genetic studies support that siblings have higher concordance rates of an ASD than with the general population, with identical twins sharing a 60% likelihood of carrying the condition. Some types of chromosomal abnormalities are linked to autistic-like behaviors, as observed in Fragile X syndrome, although many children with ASD do not have any such abnormalities. There is no credible evidence that vaccines cause ASD.

Neuroimaging studies have found some anomalies in children with ASD. Broadly speaking, there is evidence that children with autism tend to have more localized cortical functioning and weakened connectivity. In other words, the brain is less effective in communicating with itself. Support for this is found in studies that have identified less white matter in some parts of the brains of individuals with ASD. White matter represents the parts of neurons that communicate with other neurons. Gray neurons, which are the bodies of neurons, are overrepresented in children on the spectrum. It may be that this disruption of white matter and gray matter may contribute to difficulties with sensory integration, cognitive functioning, and behavioral regulation often seen in such children.

There is tremendous variability seen in children on the spectrum, therefore evaluations are useful in shedding light about your child's unique characteristics. However, this variability has made it difficult to conclusively pinpoint the exact cause of an ASD. Most likely, multiple genetic and environmental factors interact with each other. Should enough of a threshold be met, the brain experiences a neurodevelopmental change that can trigger symptoms within the developing brain.

Detection

Ever since he could first crawl, Jaime would be obsessed with spinning wheels. His first toy was a large Tonka truck and he could spend an entire afternoon just playing with the toy wheels of his truck, with little interest in actually moving the truck around or engaging with his other toys. If it wasn't a truck, it was the spinner of a board game, or a top, or anything that could turn around and around. As he became older, Jaime's interests shifted to Yu-Gi-Oh cards. He would obsessively collect them and could recite all the characters and their powers by heart. Jaime had few friends and generally was not interested in other children. He only paid his little sister attention when she got into his toys, at which point he would yell and tantrum at her. His parents ultimately decided to get him tested, initially for a speech and language disorder. However, they weren't surprised when the psychologist informed them that their son had an autistic spectrum disorder.

Early signs of an emerging ASD can be observed during the first year. Babies who do not babble, smile, make eye contact, or respond to parents early on may be at risk. Profound delays in speech during the first and second year of life is a strong risk factor for an ASD. Children who show minimal social responsiveness to caretakers are also at risk. There is also a subset of children who develop normally and then regress between their first and second year (see footnote 3). By toddlerhood, children on the spectrum often demonstrate repetitive behaviors with minimal interest in other children.

Oftentimes, your pediatrician will be the first medical professional who will take note of autistic-like behaviors and most will refer to a developmental specialist. Sometimes, children who are high functioning may go undetected for longer, and the diagnosis is not made until an educational specialist or psychologist sees the child. Like the parents in the vignette, you might not be surprised with an ASD, as the diagnosis often just confirms what was long-suspected. An ASD child might speak in an odd tone of voice, or struggle understanding social pragmatics and customs. He or she might adopt a concrete thinking style and struggle with similes, metaphors, and other figures of speech. Eye contact might be poor and social skills be in general lacking, particularly with peers. Rigid thought patterns, sensitivity to sensory information, narrow and obsessive preoccupations, and difficulty adapting to changes in the environment are also characteristic of an ASD.

Sometimes, the diagnosis does come as a surprise, particularly if your child has been functioning reasonably well. It is always best to remember that like many child neurodevelopmental disorders, an ASD just represents an extreme end of a set of symptoms and behaviors that many of us possess. Some people are less socially fluent than others, or have great interests in interesting topics. Crowds, parties, and other highly stimulating environments might be more exhausting, or disruptions of routines discomforting. These variations in personal preferences follow a more extreme pattern on the spectrum but at the end of the day, they still reflect personal preferences. Many children on the ASD grow up to lead successful, happy lives and some even become quite famous. It is always important to remember that if your child is diagnosed with an ASD, it is never your fault. The underlying root is an admixture of genes and environmental factors, but your parenting style is not part of this equation.

Not every child will exhibit the same number or severity of symptoms. One child on the spectrum might be unusually verbose and articulate, and actually enjoy social interactions even if he can come off as awkward. He might compensate for this by developing an interest in something unique that he can show off to other children. Another child might prefer a nonverbal thinking style and can be fascinated with puzzles and blocks at the expense of verbally communicating with others. Some children are anxious while others are simply disinterested, still others can learn to function at an undetectable level. There are many facets to an ASD that warrant further investigation and a detailed summary of findings can assist you in figuring out how your child thinks.

Neuropsychology of ASD

Regardless of whether your child has an ASD, he or she will be characterized by unique cognitive strengths and weaknesses. There is no real predictable pattern of neurocognitive functioning in ASD, although some researchers have noted that the now outdated Asperger's syndrome is characterized by a higher verbal intelligence (see footnote 4). As described in Chapter 4, children with intellectual disabilities will require special considerations and care, and there is a higher rate of intellectual disability among children with ASD. However, many children with ASD have near normal, normal, or even gifted intellectual abilities and for these children, a neuropsychological evaluation can provide insight on their skillsets.

Bretta's parents suspect that their daughter has an autistic spectrum disorder. However, they sought an evaluation because their daughter was beginning the third grade and they wanted to see if she would qualify for any services. The results of the evaluation confirm that Bretta has a high functioning ASD. Her intelligence was above average, in the 84th percentile, with a real strength in nonverbal abilities. The neuropsychologist noted that Bretta does struggle with integrating auditory information. This in turn has slowed down her attainment of phonics for reading, and her reading in general was quite delayed. As such, Bretta met criteria for a reading disorder. The school put in accommodations including extra time for reading and additional tutoring in phonics, in part using visual cues to leverage Bretta's nonverbal thinking style to assist with her studies.

As seen in Bretta's situation, an evaluation can explain how some of her sensory issues, which are tied to her ASD, in turn contribute to delays in phonological awareness and reading. Such evaluations should rigorously examine both expressive and receptive language skills to identify any possible delays. As executive functioning and working memory are often impacted, these also should be examined. Your child's inflexibility with new or discomforting situations might emerge through such measures. Often, children on the spectrum have difficulty seeing the "big picture" of ideas and events. In such cases, tests that look at visual-spatial abilities often reveal that such children will be overly attentive to minor details at the cost of processing the whole image. Memory is also important to examine, as differences between verbal and nonverbal abilities are often profound, although the direction of these differences can go either way. Furthermore, children on the spectrum often have substantial attentional issues and it is even possible for a high functioning child with an ASD to be misdiagnosed with ADHD (see footnote 5).

Children on the spectrum often have trouble processing emotions and reading the thoughts and feelings of others, and some tests can objectively track such deficits. During the evaluation a child might try to follow directions literally or appear confused with ambiguous instructions. Concrete thinking styles can be identified through questions that ask for the subtle meanings behind idioms and other abstract statements. Of interest, sometimes children with high intellectual functioning can perform well on these types of tests even when they qualify for an ASD, which can yield insight on their learning and problem-solving skills.

Treatment Considerations

There are multiple options available for treatment, although there is no way to effectively "cure" an ASD. One might argue that there is nothing to be cured, as ASD simply reflects a cluster of behaviors that we all exhibit to some degree or another. Many children on the spectrum are quite content when allowed to function in a manner that is comfortable for them.

> *Since the diagnosis, Evelyn enrolled her son Chris into a social skills training group. Chris went along with it but little progress seemed to be made outside of the group. She then tried to push him into joining a drama club. Chris refused so she suggested he go to a specialized camp for other children with similar gifts as him. Chris turned this down too. He preferred to spend his time interacting with his two close friends and playing role playing games with them. Evelyn felt frustrated by her son's blasé attitude towards anything social. When she asked Chris why he was so distressed with things, he looked at her and said, "Mom, you're distressed – not me."*

Many high functioning children on the spectrum are happy doing things that their parents cannot imagine doing themselves. Perhaps your child prefers to stay in his room rather than vacation in Hawaii – this doesn't necessarily mean he is depressed. He or she might be fine with low social interaction or solitary play, and that reflects some of the characteristics of an ASD. Of course, children on the spectrum may crave additional social interaction, or feel intense anxiety and worry about necessary social engagements (e.g. going to school). In such cases, therapy and social skills training may be useful methods to help your child cope.

Younger children can often benefit from behavioral therapies, particularly when such therapies are introduced at an earlier age (i.e. before five). A behavioral specialist can focus on drawing children out of their "shell" and find more reward in engaging with others.

Generally, behavioral treatments can teach children to engage in specific behaviors, but these behaviors do not necessarily generalize well. That is why it is important for parents, teachers, educators, and therapists to work together to form a cohesive multidisciplinary team. Of course, the child must be motivated as well. There is evidence that teaching social skills works best when such skills are related to interests of the child (e.g. dinosaurs, Star Wars, etc.). Sometimes, when attentional or emotional issues are a significant factor, medication can be a consideration (see footnote 6).

Prognosis

Parents will understandably be anxious about the challenges an ASD presents to their child. It is difficult to say how any particular child with an ASD will turn out – the range of outcomes are enormous. Some children eventually become indistinguishable from other adults and adolescents, while others will have severe handicaps that will require care for the rest of their lives. Most children fall in between this range and many, with care from parents, will have very good outcomes.

Psychodiagnostic testing can provide insight on long-term outcome. Children with normal to above average intelligence will likely live a more "normal" life than those with an intellectual handicap. However, even those with a disability can often have friendships and relationships and live a happy life, even if they will require someone to look after them. Additional information yielded from neuropsychological testing can provide more details on the strengths and weaknesses of your child and how these can be applied or accommodated for in the school and work environment.

FOOTNOTE 1

Very early signs include a lack of smiling and other expressions after six months of age, a lack of social reciprocity (mirroring smiles, sounds, and facial expressions) by nine months of age, a lack of babbling by one year of age, and a lack of speech by 16 months of age. Babies who develop any of these abilities but then lose them later on are also at an increased risk of developing an ASD.

FOOTNOTE 2

Some researchers will argue that risk factors that occur while the baby is in utero are among the chief environmental risk factors of developing an ASD. Such risk factors include premature births (less than 35 weeks), Apgar scores below 7, and hypoxia-related complications as risk factors. In addition, there is some evidence that advanced maternal and paternal age can increase the risk of an ASD.

FOOTNOTE 3

Childhood Disintegrative Disorder was once the term used to explain children who lose acquired abilities after approximately 3-4 years of age. Such children may regress in their speech and language, social skills, and motor skills. The exact cause of CDD remains unknown but there is evidence that a strong genetic component is involved. CDD is now subsumed under the ASD label. A related disorder, Rett's syndrome, has been taken out of the ASD as it has been found to have a unique molecular biomarker. Rett's syndrome only affects girls and is notable for a rapid loss in cognitive, sensory, and motor functions that is related to a lack of brain development.

FOOTNOTE 4

Asperger's syndrome is now considered a form of high functioning autism, although it is uniquely characterized by advanced verbal abilities at the cost of nonverbal processing. Such children may appear awkward, clumsy, and struggle with visual-spatial and mathematical abilities, but are excellent at retaining verbal information. They often have an above average vocabulary. Other forms of high functioning autism are marked by above average intellectual abilities that favor fluid reasoning over verbal intelligence. However, all children on the spectrum share struggles with social/communicative skills.

FOOTNOTE 5

Children on the spectrum often exhibit variable attention, partly because the things that they attend to are often not in line with what they are expected to attend to at home and school. Typically, ADHD should be diagnosed independently from ASD as the mechanism for the attentional problems is believed to be quite different. Furthermore, the hyperactive/impulsive behaviors often observed in ADHD are less prevalent in ASD (although they may still co-occur). One way to differentiate the two disorders is to consider the source of your child's social difficulties. Does your child understand social reciprocity but struggle in maintaining it, or do they completely lack the insight to begin with?

FOOTNOTE 6

Issues of medication should always be discussed with your medical practitioner. Some options that currently are available include antidepressants or anxiolytics when depression and/or anxiety are significant. Psychostimulants may be recommended in children who are very inattentive and/or hyperactive. Opiates are sometimes used when children engage in self-injury while antipsychotics may be prescribed when behavior is particularly difficult to control. Many of these medications come with side effects that warrant consideration.

CHAPTER 13

Concussion and Traumatic Brain Injury

Concussions and traumatic brain injuries (TBIs) in youth are major health problems in the United States. Moderate-to-severe TBIs are a leading cause of death and disability in children and adolescents. Even milder head injuries can lead to great stress and fear for the child and family. A neuropsychological evaluation is crucial to administer after a significant brain injury.

It is estimated that in the United States, almost half a million children each year are brought in for a concussion or traumatic brain injury (TBI). This does not include the many children who sustain concussions and mild head injuries that are never seen by a doctor. While the devastating impact of severe TBIs are quite apparent, there is more uncertainty when the injury is milder yet still significant. Injuries can range from very mild concussions that result in brief disorientation and confusion, to permanent brain damage, coma, and death. Generally, neuropsychological assessment is a useful tool for looking at long-term functioning and tracking cognitive changes, after the child has been medically stable for some time.

In discussing TBI, it is important to review a few terms. First, head injury refers to any injury that results in trauma to the head and/or brain. Sometimes, a child will experience a head injury (e.g. black eye) without any brain injury. Many head injuries will jar the brain, causing it to shake at the sudden movement, which can result in a concussion. Concussion is an umbrella term used to characterize bruising of the brain. Neurochemical changes occur due to the sudden disruption of the brain (see footnote 1) but there are usually no visible signs of brain damage via brain scans. Children who experience concussions may experience a brief loss of consciousness, and/or have no memory of the moments leading up to or following the injury (e.g. post-traumatic amnesia). Other children may remember the whole event but recall feeling disoriented, nauseated, or dazed.

Mild traumatic brain injury is a medical term that often refers to concussions. In a rather confusing twist, some doctors and researchers include more severe brain injuries, in which the structure of the brain has been visibly affected, as a mild traumatic brain injury although in such cases they usually refer to this as "complicated mild traumatic brain injury." Other levels of severity include moderate and severe traumatic brain injuries. The method of determining severity is usually based on an initial screening scale that a professional administers, ideally at the site of the accident (see footnote 2). While not perfect, such screeners do a reasonably good job of predicting short-term outcomes of the injury and greatly assist with treatment planning. As mentioned, neuropsychological evaluation is usually the preferred method of predicting long-term outcomes after the child has experienced some recovery.

Causes

Approximately half of all pediatric TBIs involve a motor vehicle accident. Babies can sustain head injuries from falls (see footnote

3) while older children may suffer injuries while playing sports and other recreational activities. Boys are about twice as likely to sustain a TBI compared to girls, while adolescents have the highest rates of hospitalizations and deaths, likely due to an increase of high-risk activities.

As mentioned, concussions are defined by their milder nature and typically temporary effects. Contusion is a term used for a bruising of the brain and often is the primary physical sign of a concussion. This bruising can occur both at the site of impact, and on the opposite side where the brain strikes the interior of the skull.

Diffuse axonal injury is a term used to describe disruptions of white matter in the brain. White matter consists of the neuronal tracts – or the parts of the neuron that communicate with other neurons – and sudden movement, such as the force of a car accident, can cause the white matter to tear. This tearing releases brain chemicals that can cause additional injuries and sometimes the full severity of symptoms does not emerge until later on. Traditional neuroimaging often does not pick up diffuse axonal injury, as the damage is microscopic, although some newer technologies have emerged that may assist in viewing such damage (see footnote 4).

Penetrating injuries are injuries that directly cause structural damage to the brain. As might be expected, these open-head injuries can have devastating effects on the central nervous system. Most penetrating injuries are classified as moderate or severe TBIs and the outcome is poorer, particularly when a weapon is involved.

Prognosis

The outcomes following TBI are quite variable and are contingent on the nature and severity of injury, medical intervention, and pre-injury factors such as intelligence and general cognition.

Long-term studies indicate that cognitive recovery happens the fastest during the first months after injury. Nearly all children who experience a concussion will have full recovery within two weeks after injury, with only a few experiencing symptoms longer than a month. For moderate and severe injuries, recovery usually slows down after the first three months before ultimately plateauing about a year after injury. Therefore, any gains in cognition and function are expected to happen within the first year, with only mild to minimal gains occurring afterwards. With regard to how much recovery can be expected, it is important to consider the injury's classification. Remember that severity is determined at the onset of injury based on neurological functioning and ranges from mild to moderate to severe. Mild TBIs usually result in full neurocognitive recovery within the first three months after injury. Moderate and severe TBIs result in some recovery, but generally this is to a lesser degree. As would be expected, severe TBIs have the slowest and least recovery rates after injury.

It must be emphasized that these trajectories measure neuro-cognitive abilities through testing. Cognitive recovery is a good marker of actual recovery, but cognition alone does not capture your child's actual recovery. Academic testing should also be examined to ensure that academic skills progress adequately. In addition, TBIs are incredibly stressful events that can result in emotional and psychiatric distress, even after the brain has fully resumed its functioning.

Becca is a 13-year-old girl who sustained a concussion while playing softball. She and her teammate were running towards a flyball when her teammate accidentally tripped Becca. She fell hard and was knocked out for a few seconds. At the hospital, the doctors confirmed this was a concussion. Becca had no memory of the few minutes preceding up to the injury and was very distraught. For the next few weeks, she experienced headaches, sensitivity to light, and increased irritability. Her parents pulled her out of school to allow her time to recover. Five months later, she still complained of headaches and also began to exhibit withdrawn behaviors suggesting depression. They took Becca to see her neurologist, who referred her to a neuropsychologist. Testing revealed no real cognitive weaknesses, but did identify that Becca was depressed. Furthermore, her academics were delayed by about six months, which raised concerns that she had lost some of her academic achievement following the injury.

Sometimes, children and adults who sustain mild brain injuries continue to exhibit distressing symptoms well after the three-month window of recovery. These symptoms include headaches, subjective memory loss, fatigue, irritability, depression, and anxiety. The anxiety may manifest through physical symptoms such as elevated heart rates or an exaggerated startle response. Neurologists find no evidence of brain damage and even the neuropsychological testing reveals average or better-than-average performance on testing. What exactly is happening here?

The term for this constellation of syndromes is persistent post-concussive syndrome (PPCS), a somewhat controversial diagnosis that has gained increased attention in the public eye. The actual source of PPCS remains controversial and is actively being researched at the time of this writing. Some scientists argue that PPCS largely stems from psychological factors including the trauma and stress associated with the accident, as well as the self-fulfilling prophecy that brain injury might lead to permanent brain damage. Other researchers have proposed models for a biomechanical explanation of PPCS that is currently undetectable by typical assessment tools (see footnote 5). Regardless of the source, PPCS can be a very real and stressful experience for the child suffering from it.

Neuropsychology of TBI

Pediatric TBI is a broad term for any type of trauma to the brain. As such, the neuropsychological profiles of children with TBI are quite varied and depend on premorbid functioning, the nature and severity of injury, and events that occur after the injury (e.g. treatments). However, some consistent neurocognitive patterns do emerge. Processing speed, or the speed in which we can work, generally is affected. This is in part because processing speed relies on efficient communication of multiple brain regions, one or more of which will be affected by the injury. Attention and executive functioning weaknesses emerge for similar reasons; both are reliant on multiple regions of the brain (with an emphasis on the frontal lobes) and so disruption of any of these regions will affect these domains.

Other aspects of cognition may be affected. Injury to the parietal lobes can impact visual-spatial skills, while some frontal lobe damage can impact language. Memory is most likely to be diminished when the temporal lobes are injured, although disruptions in attention and executive functioning can indirectly affect memory. There is some evidence that children may lose efficiency in visual or verbal memory with comparative sparing in the other form of memory, although it is difficult to determine why this happens.

More severe injuries can lead to permanent cognitive changes that are often expressed through a decline in IQ. Generally, verbal intelligence is more resilient to brain injury although it can also decline in some cases, while fluid and visual-spatial intelligence are more vulnerable. Severe injuries can also lead to motor and sensory deficits that are often identified during the neurological examination.

Treatment Strategies

When your child has sustained a mild injury such as a concussion, it often is prudent to seek medical help. This is because concussions can lead to hematomas (i.e. brain bleeds) which do not immediately present with symptoms. If your child begins to become drowsy, has a worsening headache, becomes dizzy and nauseous, or experiences any loss of consciousness, confusion, or amnesia about the event, then an immediate visit to a doctor is essential. Mild headaches that

to see her neurologist, who referred her to a neuropsychologist. Testing revealed no real cognitive weaknesses, but did identify that Becca was depressed. Furthermore, her academics were delayed by about six months, which raised concerns that she had lost some of her academic achievement following the injury.

Sometimes, children and adults who sustain mild brain injuries continue to exhibit distressing symptoms well after the three-month window of recovery. These symptoms include headaches, subjective memory loss, fatigue, irritability, depression, and anxiety. The anxiety may manifest through physical symptoms such as elevated heart rates or an exaggerated startle response. Neurologists find no evidence of brain damage and even the neuropsychological testing reveals average or better-than-average performance on testing. What exactly is happening here?

The term for this constellation of syndromes is persistent post-concussive syndrome (PPCS), a somewhat controversial diagnosis that has gained increased attention in the public eye. The actual source of PPCS remains controversial and is actively being researched at the time of this writing. Some scientists argue that PPCS largely stems from psychological factors including the trauma and stress associated with the accident, as well as the self-fulfilling prophecy that brain injury might lead to permanent brain damage. Other researchers have proposed models for a biomechanical explanation of PPCS that is currently undetectable by typical assessment tools (see footnote 5). Regardless of the source, PPCS can be a very real and stressful experience for the child suffering from it.

Neuropsychology of TBI

Pediatric TBI is a broad term for any type of trauma to the brain. As such, the neuropsychological profiles of children with TBI are quite varied and depend on premorbid functioning, the nature and severity go away shortly after the injury are less of a concern. However, if you have any doubt or concerns, then a medical checkup is paramount.

Once a child is stabilized, the best short-term treatment for concussion is to rest. A second concussion shortly after the first increases the risk for additional injury (see footnote 6) so children should avoid any activities that will put them at risk. It is also recommended that children avoid mentally stimulating activities, such as playing video games or using a SmartPhone. Sometimes doctors recommend that schoolwork be reduced to help the child recover. However, too much neglect of schoolwork can have unintentional consequences as well, so a balance must be met.

There is also some evidence that children are more likely to experience long-term symptoms when they are in a high-stress environment. Concussions require rest to recover, although the concussion itself should not be emphasized as a serious or debilitating injury, as this can lead to undue stress and anxiety. As most children recover within two weeks, those who continue to experience symptoms should not remain bedridden at the expense of their academic and social development. You should discuss a treatment plan with your doctors should you have a child who may be at risk for a persistent post-concussive syndrome.

When an injury is more severe, the risk of long-term disability is real. Unfortunately, there is no way to definitively know how much your child will recover. A neuropsychological evaluation can provide an estimate and cognitive gains over time provide a measure of recovery. Severe injuries can sometimes result in permanent disability and in such cases, treatment should shift towards accommodating and providing the best quality of life for your child.

I want to reassure that most TBIs are mild in nature, with a few that are moderate and even fewer that are severe. Most children who sustain a concussion fully recover, and even the subset who develop post-concussive symptoms will usually improve over time. In the cases where moderate and severe injuries have caused a permanent change, there are many resources available for parents seeking aid. It is vital to encourage and praise a child's gains and involve friends, the school and the greater community as much as possible. Child and family counselors can help prepare the family for necessary adjustments and some professionals specialize with TBI.

There is a type of therapy called cognitive rehabilitation, which is specifically aimed to help individuals with cognitive deficits. While brain-training exercises may have some utility (see footnote 7), the most evidence-based methods of rehabilitation involve accepting and coping with losses, and developing cognitive strategies that can overcome the losses.

FOOTNOTE 1

Concussion causes direct trauma to the brain, and indirect trauma from altered blood flow due to the injury. When the brain is impacted, microstructural changes in the neurons make it more difficult for cells to regulate themselves. Neurochemical changes occur in which neuronal equilibrium is thrown off. Glutamate, an excitatory neurotransmitter, is released in excess, which can be toxic to the brain. Furthermore, the injured cells require more energy as they try to recover, which leads to an increased metabolic demand of the affected area. Exertion during this recovery period will further tax the demand and exacerbate concussion symptoms.

change, there are many resources available for parents seeking aid. It is vital to encourage and praise a child's gains and involve friends, the school and the greater community as much as possible. Child and family counselors can help prepare the family for necessary adjustments and some professionals specialize with TBI.

There is a type of therapy called cognitive rehabilitation, which is specifically aimed to help individuals with cognitive deficits. While brain-training exercises may have some utility (see footnote 7), the most evidence-based methods of rehabilitation involve accepting and coping with losses, and developing cognitive strategies that can overcome the losses.

FOOTNOTE 1

Concussion causes direct trauma to the brain, and indirect trauma from altered blood flow due to the injury. When the brain is impacted, microstructural changes in the neurons make it more difficult for cells to regulate themselves. Neurochemical changes occur in which neuronal equilibrium is thrown off. Glutamate, an excitatory neurotransmitter, is released in excess, which can be toxic to the brain. Furthermore, the injured cells require more energy as they try to recover, which leads to an increased metabolic demand of the affected area. Exertion during this recovery period will further tax the demand and exacerbate concussion symptoms.

go away shortly after the injury are less of a concern. However, if you have any doubt or concerns, then a medical checkup is paramount.

Once a child is stabilized, the best short-term treatment for concussion is to rest. A second concussion shortly after the first increases the risk for additional injury (see footnote 6) so children should avoid any activities that will put them at risk. It is also recommended that children avoid mentally stimulating activities, such as playing video games or using a SmartPhone. Sometimes doctors recommend that schoolwork be reduced to help the child recover. However, too much neglect of schoolwork can have unintentional consequences as well, so a balance must be met.

There is also some evidence that children are more likely to experience long-term symptoms when they are in a high-stress environment. Concussions require rest to recover, although the concussion itself should not be emphasized as a serious or debilitating injury, as this can lead to undue stress and anxiety. As most children recover within two weeks, those who continue to experience symptoms should not remain bedridden at the expense of their academic and social development. You should discuss a treatment plan with your doctors should you have a child who may be at risk for a persistent post-concussive syndrome.

When an injury is more severe, the risk of long-term disability is real. Unfortunately, there is no way to definitively know how much your child will recover. A neuropsychological evaluation can provide an estimate and cognitive gains over time provide a measure of recovery. Severe injuries can sometimes result in permanent disability and in such cases, treatment should shift towards accommodating and providing the best quality of life for your child.

I want to reassure that most TBIs are mild in nature, with a few that are moderate and even fewer that are severe. Most children who sustain a concussion fully recover, and even the subset who develop post-concussive symptoms will usually improve over time. In the cases where moderate and severe injuries have caused a permanent

FOOTNOTE 2

One of the more widely used measures is the Glasgow Coma Scale. This scale assesses behavioral functioning after the injury including motor, verbal, and eye opening abilities. Scores for each of these are derived and then summed to provide an estimate of severity, which is categorized as either mild, moderate, or severe. While the Glasgow Coma Scale is principally used as a preliminary estimate of severity that is later refined by neuroimaging and neuropsychological testing, it can be reasonably predictive of future functioning on its own. Additional markers of severity include length of unconsciousness (<30 minutes to be mild) and length of memory loss (<24 hours to be mild).

FOOTNOTE 3

Infant falls are a common reason for ER visits and with good reason. Generally, falls over three feet are of concern and warrant medical intervention. If at any point the infant appears to be in pain, bleeds, or becomes unresponsive, an immediate consultation with your pediatrician or a trip to the ER is warranted.

FOOTNOTE 4

Diffuse tensor imaging (DTI) is a sophisticated form of brain imaging that examines the molecular structure of water surrounding white matter. Based on the disruption of these molecules, the structure of white matter can be estimated and then mapped out. DTI is therefore a useful way to detect white matter changes secondary to traumatic brain injury. Due to its cost and novelty, it is primarily used in research studies, although increased interest in clinical application is growing.

FOOTNOTE 5

PPCS is still poorly understood, but one hypothesis posits that the autonomic nervous system (ANS) is involved. The ANS regulates our "flight or fight" mechanism and influences heart rate, respiration, and muscle contractions, among other autonomic functions. Children and adults with PPCS often have a hypersensitive ANS, although whether this is causative (e.g. due to microstructural damage to the systems around the ANS) or simply a symptom of PPCS remains a debate.

FOOTNOTE 6

After a concussion, the brain devotes increased resources to repairing the damaged cells, often leading to full recovery. However, a second concussion *anywhere* in the brain will interrupt this sequence and further tax the brain. Like any organism that uses energy, the brain only has a finite supply of resources and ability and too much stress can lead to exacerbation of the injury. A rare and someone controversial condition is second impact syndrome, in which a second concussion following the first leads to sudden brain swelling and death. Regardless, there is evidence that multiple concussions over time can lead to long-term brain damage.

FOOTNOTE 7

So-called brain training tools use computerized tasks to "strengthen" the brain, much like weights can strengthen the muscles. Controlled studies generally show that any gains from such tools are likely placebo in nature, and at best improve one's ability to complete the tasks themselves. However, there is also evidence to suggest that *not* using your brain can be harmful – while this is particularly relevant in the dementia literature, it stands to reason that children who have sustained TBIs should try to remain as mentally and physically active as their injuries safely permit.

CHAPTER 14

Other Neurological Syndromes

This chapter reviews some of the other neurological syndromes that impact the central nervous system in children and adolescents. This review serves as a brief introduction to conditions that may warrant further investigation.

Neuropsychological evaluations are routinely administered when there is a suspected or identified neurological condition. Such conditions often impact cognition and behavior and the same condition in two different children can result in very different outcomes. As such, evaluations can help take a known neurological illness or syndrome and make it much more understandable in terms of your child's cognitive and emotional health. Neuropsychological evaluations are often administered at the hospital where the child has been admitted. Sometimes, reevaluations in outpatient and private practice settings are warranted to help the child prepare for future academics as well as track any patterns of recovery or loss.

Anoxic Brain Injury

An anoxic brain injury (ABI) occurs when the brain has an inadequate supply of oxygen. This can occur due to birth complications, toxins, cardiac arrest, drowning, and other situations in which oxygen is prevented from traveling to the brain. ABI can result in temporary or permanent brain damage and in extreme cases individuals will be in a permanent coma or die. As with traumatic brain injury, the outcomes of ABI vary depending on the nature and severity of injury. Typically, short-term memory loss is a common consequence as the parts of the brain responsible for learning new information are very dependent on oxygen. Other symptoms include impairments in executive functioning, behavioral and emotional changes, and loss of sensory and motor functions.

ABI is typically diagnosed through neuroimaging and blood tests. Neuropsychological testing is appropriate after the child has stabilized to ascertain loss of functioning and track cognitive recovery over time. Recovery patterns are similar to those observed in TBI (see Chapter 14), with acute gains early on and slower recovery up until one year, at which point further recovery is rare.

Seizure Disorders

Seizure disorders are a product of central nervous system damage, and can stem from either neurodevelopmental (e.g. metabolic disorders, spina bifida) or external factors (e.g. viruses, traumatic brain injury). Seizures refer to individual episodes in which the brain begins to fire neurons in a seemingly random manner. A single seizure does not necessarily indicate a seizure disorder, as approximately 70% of children experience only one episode in their lives. If a second seizure occurs, it is usually within a year of the first seizure.

Seizures can be classified by their semiology, or the behavioral signs and symptoms of the episode. The classic presentation involves the whole body shaking and jerking with associated loss of consciousness, complete loss of voluntary motor control, and no memory of the event afterwards. These seizures are referred to as "tonic-clonic" seizures or more classically, "grand mal" seizures. Tonic-clonic seizures reflect whole brain activity.

Partial seizures refer to localized seizures that can be linked to a specific lesion in the brain. These seizures may or may not be associated with a loss of consciousness and may only affect one side of the body. A third type of seizure is absence seizures, which result in an abrupt loss of consciousness with minimal motor or sensory loss. Children with absence seizures often are unaware that they had a seizure and adults may perceive them to be "daydreaming" or spaced out. In some cases, if left untreated partial and absence seizures can progress to a tonic-clonic seizure.

Seizure disorders are primarily diagnosed with EEG, a neuro-imaging device that measures electrical brain activity. Associated behavioral observations refine the nature of the seizures. Sometimes there are things that trigger seizures (e.g. bright lights, lack of sleep) while other times they only occur at certain points of time (e.g. while sleeping). Children may report headaches, auras, or strange feelings prior to the onset of a seizure and often experience headaches, drowsiness, and fatigue after a seizure, particularly when it was severe.

Neuropsychological outcomes of seizures vary, from no cognitive impairment to progressive loss of functioning in severe cases. Academic delays often are present, both due to cognitive loss as well as associated absence from school due to the illness. Often children present with behavioral and emotional issues, particularly when executive functioning is affected. Ongoing neuropsychological assessment is crucial to obtain measures of cognitive change over time. Cognition can improve, particularly as the seizure disorder is treated and stabilized. Frequent seizures and tonic-clonic seizures are associated with poorer outcomes.

Antiepileptic drugs are crucial for managing seizures. Unfortunately, these can come with side effects, cognitive and behavioral problems among them. Children can attenuate to medication regimes and the prevention of additional seizures takes precedence over side effects of any medications that are found to be effective. In rarer cases, neurosurgery is an option when medication has shown to be ineffective and when the seizures have been localized to one side of the brain.

Genetic Disorders

Genetic disorders refer to disorders that emerge due to chromosomal abnormalities. Many genetic disorders have profound effects on cognition, behavior, and physical health although with care, many children can still live enriched lives. The most widely known genetic disorder is Down syndrome, in which children possess an extra copy of chromosome 21. Down syndrome can be inherited although it typically emerges spontaneously. Children with Down syndrome have mild to severe intellectual loss. Physical features include a small head, folds in their eyes, a flattened nose, and increased risk of medical complications. Such children need a supportive environment to thrive. Depending on their level of intelligence, they may achieve a degree of independence and self-care as they age. Sometimes, such children can transition into adults who can maintain work and relationships. Unfortunately, adults with Down syndrome often live shorter lives due to the associated medical complications.

Another chromosomal disorder is Klinefelter syndrome, in which an extra X chromosome is present. It exclusively affects men and results in a taller stature and smaller sexual organs. There are cognitive and behavioral problems as well as increased anxiety and passivity that can impact peer-relationships. Intelligence is usually preserved, but language and motor delays are often present. Sometime, children with Klinefelter syndrome are never diagnosed and simply transition to normal adults in society. However, hormonal therapy can assist with some of the symptoms if an early diagnosis is made.

Fragile X syndrome refers to a mutation of the X chromosome. It can happen with both girls and boys and is linked to cognitive impairment ranging from normal intelligence with mild cognitive issues to profound impairment. Boys in particular are at an increased risk of intellectual disability, perhaps because they possess only one X chromosome. Unlike Down syndrome, Fragile X is not as immediately identifiable and children may appear to progress normally until after the age of 5, at which point noted declines are observed. Physical signs of the condition include enlarged ears and a long face, although genetic testing is required to establish the diagnosis. As Fragile X syndrome can impact sensory integration and social skills, many children with this condition are eventually diagnosed with a co-occurring autistic spectrum disorder.

22q11.2 Deletion Syndrome is caused by the deletion of a small segment of chromosome 22. It can result in a wide variety of symptoms including heart defects, reduced immune system functionality, and cognitive/learning issues. Children with this syndrome are also at increased risk of developing schizophrenia later in life. Neuropsychological profiles generally find better verbal intelligence over nonverbal intelligence, although language skills are delayed. Autistic-like symptoms may be present. Some children can attend normal schools (with accommodations) while others will require special education.

Many other genetically related conditions exist. Some directly affect metabolism, such as phenylketonuria (PKU), in which the body cannot break down a protein called phenylalanine. As phenylalanine is prevalent in many foods, a strict diet is essential to avoid significant cognitive impairment. Other conditions fall under the neurocutaneous syndromes, in which the skin is affected. For example, neurofibromatosis results in chronic tumors in the nervous system, most which are benign but some develop into cancer. Tumors often appear on or under the skin and severity can range from mild freckles and spots to severe deformities. IQ can range from disabled to gifted, although some learning deficits in language and visual-spatial skills often are present. Social and emotional problems often emerge because of teasing and isolation due to the skin condition.

Cerebral Palsy

Cerebral palsy is a neurodevelopmental disorder that is characterized by damage to the motor system. It is not a singular disorder but rather a syndrome that arises from a number of sources and shares a common disruption in movement. This damage usually happens at some point between prenatal development and the age of three and may be caused by birth complications, disease, and traumatic brain injury. Children with cerebral palsy have poor control of their voluntary movements, which may result in spastic and exaggerated movements. Although this condition is primarily associated with the motor system, co-occurring damage to neighboring parts of the brain may result in cognitive and learning disabilities. Children with this condition are at an increased risk of meeting criteria for an intellectual disability, ADHD, and learning disabilities.

Toxic Exposures

There are a number of toxic substances that can interfere with brain functioning. Children are particularly vulnerable to such toxins, in part because their brains are still developing. Certain elements such as lead, mercury, and radioactive metals can result in permanent brain damage. Children who experience such brain damage often have problems with working memory, attention, processing speed, and executive functioning and may develop academic, behavioral, and emotional disorders. As might be expected, prenatal exposure can be particularly harmful for the developing fetus.

Prenatal exposure to drugs and alcohol can also have long-lasting effects. Children who are exposed to alcohol in the womb are at risk for developing with Fetal Alcohol Syndrome (FAS) or a related disorder. Studies suggest that heavy (i.e. daily) maternal alcohol use during the first and second trimesters is a particular risk factor. Although we still do not fully understand the mechanism behind alcohol's devastating effects on the developing fetus, we are aware of the results which include decreased brain size, intellectual disability, and cognitive deficits. Children with FAS often have distinct facial features including a small upper lip, flattened face, and a smooth ridge between the nose and upper lip. Growth is usually delayed as well.

Some children who are exposed to alcohol in the womb develop less severe variants of FAS. These variants are usually referred to as "Fetal alcohol spectrum disorder" (FASD) and generally result in one or more symptoms of the classic FAS without meeting the full criteria. Some children with FASD primarily have cognitive problems with few if any physical deformities, while others might be intellectually normal yet have other birth effects that interfere with their physical health.

Children exposed to cocaine are also at an increased risk of cognitive delays and often experience academic and behavioral difficulties at school. Issues with attention and executive functioning are often observed. The severity of such deficits vary and studies suggest that cocaine-exposure, alongside other factors such as maternal health, prenatal care, and the child's early environment, all play a role in increasing the risk of cognitive and behavioral problems later in life.

Cancer

Although childhood cancer is rare, it does occur and the two most common types are leukemia and brain tumors. Leukemia is a type of cancer that affects white blood cells. Treatment for childhood leukemia usually involves chemotherapy, and there is evidence that chemotherapy can affect cognition. Post-chemotherapy cognitive impairment, or "chemo brain" is a syndrome used to describe the cognitive impairment experienced after treatment. Children who are treated for leukemia often have slowed processing speed and weaknesses in attention, memory, and visual-spatial skills. Sometimes, radiation therapy is used to treat leukemia and this too can have long-lasting effects on cognition.

Brain tumors directly impact cognition by displacing brain tissue and indirectly do so through radiation therapy, which is a common treatment. Radiation therapy can have late effects on cognition and children require careful monitoring and frequent follow-up to track their cognitive and academic progress.

Summary

The above neurological syndromes are often very challenging for the child and the family. Even after the initial stages, where the focus is on the child's survival, there remain medical concerns and the associated cognitive, emotional, and behavioral issues that often emerge once the child is stabilized. Neuropsychologists can assist not just in identifying the cognitive changes that your child has experienced, but also aid in providing emotional support and guidance for the family. As always, we serve as part of your treatment team in helping you and your child adjust to these challenges in life and work to provide the resources available to help work through these difficult situations.

CHAPTER 15

The Holistic Child

The last few chapters were about the common diagnoses that are the reason for or the result of a neuropsychological evaluation. Most of these disorders come with associated cognitive weaknesses that necessitate interventions and accommodations. However, an assessment will also bring to light your child's strengths. This chapter discusses what those might be and the possible implications for your child's future.

An important benefit of a thorough evaluation is the ability to create a "roadmap" of your child's learning style that can help guide you and your child through this increasingly complex world that we live in. We all have to process information through numerous methods and just as some people are better sprinters while others are endurance runners, we do not all share the same cognitive style. Outlining these styles for you and your child is perhaps the most unique service a neuropsychologist can provide for you. I encourage readers to review Chapters 4 and 5, which provide an overview of IQ and neuropsychological domains.

Intelligence

As reviewed in chapter 4 there are several criticisms about IQ scores, most of which concern the generalizability of such scores to actual intelligence. There are issues with measurement error, test selection, and interpretation of scores in the context of cognitive/learning disabilities that could generate a lower IQ score without actually indicating a lower intelligence.

With that said, when an IQ test is used and interpreted appropriately within the context of a neuropsychological evaluation, they can be informative about a child's abilities. Some of the individual subtests within a battery are on their own quite predictive of the estimated full scale IQ of older children (see footnote 1), and children who score well on these tests may have higher intelligence than what their actual IQ score suggests.

If we use the analogy of accumulated knowledge being a liquid, then actual intelligence is the size of the reservoir that holds this liquid. When the reservoir is too small, then no matter how much you pour into it, knowledge will spill out. Taking what we reviewed in Chapter 4, an "average" sized reservoir is quite sufficient for many of the things expected in life. Larger reservoirs may confer additional benefits, but also have their own issues to consider. In general, however, children with low average to high average intelligence have the ability to complete a college education if not more. Therefore, it is still worth learning about your child's IQ, with the caveat that the full scale IQ score should not be accepted at face value and a thorough discussion with the neuropsychologist is recommended to fully appreciate your child's performance on an IQ test.

To summarize, IQ scores are not always great representations of intelligence, although sometimes specific IQ subtests can provide a rough estimate of your child's overall potential to learn and apply information in a functional way. Very low intelligence does limit what your child can do, while average intelligence conveys potential to perform many academic milestones expected of children up through college. Furthermore, above average intelligence may further widen the options available to your child both now and in the future.

Visual/Auditory Processing

We all process information using our senses. While our touch, smell, and taste senses are certainly relevant for growth and development, vision and hearing are predominant in the academic environment. Evaluations separately consider how children process auditory and visual information and which method is most efficient for their learning.

Auditory information begins in the ears where receptor cells detect sound waves which are then converted into neural signals. Some children are particularly adept at handling multiple incoming auditory stimuli, which allows them to quickly integrate auditory information in both ears into cognitive interpretation. Auditory processing can take the form of recognizing auditory patterns (e.g. speech and music), discriminating relevant sounds from background noise, and discriminating similar sounds from each other. Another form of auditory processing is prosodic interpretation, or the ability to pick up the meanings of words based on changes in intonation, pitch, and rate.

These individual abilities usually work in synch and it is easy to see how children who are particularly adept at auditory processing can develop numerous skills in life. Children with strong auditory processing may have inherent musical talent as they have a natural proclivity towards pitch, rhythm, tone, and other critical features of music. They may become excellent orators as they can pick up the subtler aspects of speech. Auditory processing also carries over to general social fluency as speech is so inherently connected to how we communicate. Furthermore, children with strong auditory processing may have an advantage in reading, as auditory processing is crucial for phonological processing. Even children who are behind in reading for other reasons might be able to leverage their natural auditory abilities to help them catch up (see footnote 2). Strong auditory processing skills often transfer into strong language, verbal memory, and verbal intelligence abilities as well.

Visual processing starts with the eye, which detects light that is converted into neural information that is then processed in the brain. Just like with sounds, multiple aspects of vision are simultaneously processed into the gestalt "whole" of what we see and interpret. Some children can identify key figures amongst a visually complex background without difficulty. They might able to recognize the visual whole of something just by seeing a part of it (e.g. in seeing half a trunk and an ear, one might recognize the elephant). Other children might recognize that there are certain constancies in contours and shapes that give rise to more complex figures, and can identify patterns based on these constancies (e.g. recognizing that certain types of four-sided figures are rectangles or that rectangles are key features in certain types of architecture).

A related feature of visual processing is visual-motor processing, which requires an effective synchronizing between the hand and the eye. Children who have strong visual-motor skills can not only process the subtleties of visual information well, but can also transfer visual information into motor output for a specific purpose, whether it be tracing, copying, building, or something else. Such children naturally have skills in both visual and motor abilities, and furthermore are skilled in combining these two abilities for a higher cognitive purpose.

Children with strong visual processing skills are often adept at pattern recognition. They might be able to find key relevant features in a sea of visual information for some purpose. This may emerge in the social context, where they might take in a room of people and immediately come to accurate conclusions about the situation based on visual cues such as body language. Such children might appear to have a strong "intuition," which ties in with their ability to process a complex scene almost instantaneously and pick up what is really going on. Many children who are strong with visual processing have an advantage in the visual arts such as drawing, painting, and sculpture, as well as athletics. They may be drawn towards graphic design, architecture, or other highly visual jobs. Visual processing is also crucial for reading, and children who can identify wholes from parts can often figure out the reading of a word just by looking at a few key features (e.g. first and last letters). Finally, strong visual processing skills often predict strong fluid reasoning, visual memory, and visual–spatial abilities.

Working Memory

Working memory is one of the most well studied cognitive constructs in neuroscience (see footnote 3). Children with strong working memory have the ability to hold and manipulate information in their minds for a longer period of time than most individuals. This assists with learning, memorization, and problem solving. Think of a lecture hall: students must listen to a professor talk at length about the subject at hand. Those with stronger working memory can hold what the professor said in their minds longer, which eases their ability to follow along, write down notes, and synthesize new concepts with already learned information. Outside the lecture hall, reading comprehension itself depends in part on working memory; children who can read a long text and then integrate the information with prior knowledge are at an advantage in learning.

Working memory is subdivided into several components, including a phonological loop (e.g. auditory), visual-spatial sketchpad (e.g. visual), and a central executive component which maintains and manipulates the incoming information for processing into long-term storage. While a strong working memory does correlate with overall intelligence, it is best to view it as a separate aspect of cognition that relates to learning, particularly of more complex concepts versus simple rote information. Good working memory facilitates faster learning, but children with weaknesses in working memory can still display remarkable overall intelligence. Children with efficient working memory may simply be more efficient in learning and mastering new concepts, and may be perceived by others as a quick learner or a fast problem-solver.

Processing Speed

Like working memory, processing speed is one of the "engines" of the mind that drive our ability to acquire new information. However, unlike working memory, our processing speed is more automatic in nature; there is less conscious "effort" involved in processing speed. Processing speed refers to the speed at which we can move through material in an effective manner. Many children might appear "fast" but do so at the expense of learning; the child with fast processing speed might be able to read through a book, think on their feet, or react to external stimuli at a rate faster than most children.

In order for children to have fast processing speed, many other components must line up as well. Sensory processing and sustained attention and concentration are all core factors of many processing speed tests. Some tests also require fine motor speed and working memory for optimal performance (see footnote 4) and academic fluency tests require automaticity of the task at hand (e.g. reading) along with processing speed. Therefore, fast processing speed is an excellent sign of general cognitive efficiency that will generalize to many other domains.

Children with fast processing speed can often learn quickly, although high processing scores with low working memory scores might suggest that they can progress through simple tasks easily, but have trouble remembering more complex tasks. Children who are naturally fast often become accustomed to working quickly; however, even the brightest children will make careless errors if they perform too quickly. Sometimes, naturally fast children struggle more in high school and college, where raw speed is less of a critical factor for academic success.

Verbal/Nonverbal Memory

Some children think more verbally, with words while others prefer nonverbal information like contours, shapes, color and movement. The term 'visual memory' is sometimes used erroneously to describe nonverbal memory, as visual stimuli can often be recalled through verbal prompting ("this looks like a red square over a blue box, like a police car"). Some children can thus harness their strong verbal skills to excel with nonverbal material.

Children with strong verbal or nonverbal abilities naturally will function well in environments that promote the same forms of information. Children with natural skills in verbal memory can have advantages in reading, spelling, and writing. They might be skilled orators. Such children may be more drawn towards jobs that rely heavily on writing, reading, or speaking, such as the English arts, law, and politics. Children with excellent nonverbal memory may do well with abstract thinking, the arts, and visually heavy material and may be drawn towards similar paths as children with strong visual processing speed. Some children have a balance in both abilities, which speaks well to their mental flexibility and broadens the types of tasks and jobs that they might enjoy.

Executive Functioning

In the hierarchy of neuropsychological domains, executive functioning is firmly at the top. The tasks that require executive functioning rely on numerous cortical and subcortical circuits for efficient processing, and so excellent executive functioning across all the various scores administered often conveys good brain "health." That is not to say that a child with great executive functioning might not struggle in a lower cognitive process, but it does suggest that they have found ways to compensate for this struggle.

As reviewed in Chapter 5, executive functioning is an umbrella term that refers to abilities that are dependent on the prefrontal cortex. Such abilities include planning, abstract thinking, response inhibition, attentional switching (e.g. multitasking), and problem solving. Children who excel in lower processes might have advantages with the executive processes; for example, excellent attentional switching requires good sustained attention and working memory. In fact, the central executive component of working memory is directly tied to the prefrontal cortex and can be considered an executive functioning ability.

Strong executive skills in individual abilities often directly relate to day-to-day living. A child who performs well on response inhibition tests can likely refrain from acting out in situations where it is not warranted. High scores on set-switching tests suggest that the child is able to move from activity to activity without getting "stuck" or overly focused on a specific task. Strengths in attentional switching convey similar benefits, along with the ability to work on one thing, then another, and back again, which may be referred as multi-tasking (see footnote 5). As earlier described, high scores across all executive functioning tests is an indicator that your child's brain is functioning well across multiple levels.

The Holistic Child

A neuropsychological assessment can provide clues on how your child best functions, but it is only a small piece of the puzzle in unlocking your child's ultimate potential. Cognition is dynamic and can fluctuate and change based on other factors. Physical health, for instance, can affect attention, memory, and executive functioning. Adequate nutrition is crucial for optimal brain development that in turn impacts intelligence and general cognitive abilities. Children's environments and support systems play key roles in how they develop and how they use the skills that they have acquired. Emotional health is of utmost importance; a child might have all the intelligence, working memory, and academic skills in the world and yet little of that matters if he is so depressed he can barely get out of bed.

Academics are important, but along with acquiring skills in reading, writing, and mathematics, other skills are important to develop as well. Often we measure ourselves by numbers and by data, and an evaluation certainly contributes to this. However, real life goes beyond a score sheet and a diagnosis. There is recent interest in developing a scientific method of capturing what we view as a "happy" and "fulfilling" life (see footnote 6), which depends in large part on one's personal relationships.

Of all the factors that contribute to your child's growth and development, you, the parent is the most important. The neuropsychological evaluation, along with the services of other professionals and educators, can assist and guide you as you help your child navigate through life and achieve their potential as a human being. In this endeavor I wish you the very best.

FOOTNOTE 1

Estimating premorbid IQ in children is more challenging than estimating it in adults, as children are still acquiring the basic skills that will eventually serve as "anchor points" of intelligence after they grow up. It is in fact very difficult to use any single score to estimate IQ in children who are under 9 years of age. In such cases, parental level of education serves as a better estimate than any test score. In older children, there is some literature that suggests that vocabulary and matrix reasoning (i.e. pattern recognition) tests are the most "stable" scores that are resilient to other cognitive factors. This is in part because such tests are untimed and tap into a broad knowledge base.

FOOTNOTE 2

Reading requires both visual and auditory abilities, the former to process written information and the latter to develop adequate phonics and vocabulary. Some children struggle in reading because they have trouble visually processing the individual letters and words; they may benefit from focused phonological tutoring as their strong auditory skills enable them to quickly learn how words are pronounced. However, they still struggle in transferring phonics into the corresponding visual representations. There is reason to believe that the English language is particularly difficult because so many words violate conventional phonetical structure.

FOOTNOTE 3

Working memory is somewhat unique in that it has been linked to genotypes, neurotransmitters, and neuronal networks in studying disease patterns. For example, studies show that individuals with a variation of the Catechol-O-methyl transferase (COMT) gene have difficulty breaking down dopamine, a neurotransmitter that is crucial for attention, motivation, and pleasure. Excess dopamine in turn is linked to increased frontal lobe dysfunction, poorer working memory, and psychosis. The frontal lobe's role in modulating working memory is well established, with some models proposing three distinct circuits that are all involved in different aspects of this construct.

FOOTNOTE 4

Wechsler processing subtests typically include a cancellation task, a symbol search task, and a coding task. The former two are relatively straightforward in that the patient has to scan a page for target items while ignoring non-target items. Coding is more complex as it requires the patient to convert numbers into their correspondence abstract symbols and code the symbols as quickly as possible. This requires working memory, fine motor abilities, and processing speed, and children who perform well on the other two subtests while underperforming on coding may actually exhibit weaknesses in functions other than processing speed.

FOOTNOTE 5

Many of us (this author included) take pride in multitasking. While it is true that some individuals might be able to multitask better than others, there remains a harsh truth: we actually cannot pay attention to two things simultaneously. Multitasking really reflects rapid attentional switching between various tasks, but we still inevitably are paying attention to just one thing at a time. This can still seem like seamless simultaneously processing, but we do lose information when we try to do multiple things at once. Food for thought if you think you can study with the television on, or write a paper next to a crying baby!

FOOTNOTE 6

Positive psychology is a discipline of psychology dedicated to studying the processes of human happiness. This field studies ideas such as a meaningful and fulfilling life, optimism, virtues, and behaviors that facilitate all of the above. Many studies support that relationships, health, and environment are all significant contributions to "happiness." Interested readers are encouraged to read Martin Seligman's work for more detail.

Appendix
The History and State of Clinical Neuropsychology

This chapter provides a background on the formative years of clinical neuropsychology and how it has evolved to the science that it is today. Readers who have a curiosity about the field might find this chapter interesting, although unlike other chapters it is not as directly applicable to you or your child.

Clinical neuropsychology is a specialty in psychology that is concerned with brain-behavior relationships. In other words, clinical neuropsychologists examine how the neurological and psychological state of the brain translates into behavior. By behavior, we usually refer to behavior in day-to-day functioning, but we actually observe or test behaviors within a very circumscribed setting – during the evaluation. While someone might report forgetting their car keys all the time, or struggle with driving, or suddenly failing in math class, these concerns are usually not directly observable within the timeframe of the evaluation. Therefore, neuropsychologists rely on a series of test batteries to obtain a snapshot of the patient's functioning.

Our tests are designed to measure a number of different brain functions. For example, one test might ask the patient to remember a series of short stories, while another test tracks visual attention on a computer screen. Often, these types of tests are referred as "cognitive" or "neurocognitive" tests. By cognition, we are referring to an aspect of human thinking that allows us to function in our lives. As described in Chapters 4 and 5, there are many cognitive tests that measure the brain. However, at the end of it all, our tests primarily measure *behavior.* This is because tests can only capture performance, and one's performance is measured on how they behave during these tests. I encourage all readers to keep this in mind as they move forward.

Neuropsychology emerged from discoveries in psychology and medicine in the early to mid-1800's. Interest in brain-behavior relationships are longstanding and predate the 20th century, but a boom in experimental research occurred alongside the industrial revolution. Pioneers such as Paul Broca and Hermann von Helmholtz established that brain structures can directly influenced human behavior (see footnote 1) and a new generation of experimental researchers developed interest in further looking at this.

Some of the first psychologists were primarily experimenters who worked in laboratories across the country. While not classically thought of as a neuropsychologist, the German psychologist William Wundt is regarded as one of the founders of experimental psychology and much of his research captures aspects of clinical assessment today. For example, he was interested in how reaction time served as a measure of nerve conduction speed. Reaction time, while no longer specifically looked at as a measure of "nerve conductance," remains a measure of interest by psychologists today.

By the late 1800s and early 1900s, several of Wundt's students had started their own laboratories aimed at capturing other aspects of human behavior. William James and his student, Mary Whiton Calkins, were pioneers in studying attention and memory whose work laid the groundwork for some of the tests that are used today. In New York City, Hans-Lukas Teuber acknowledged the potential in merging experimental psychology with neurology, perhaps being the first to officially refer to this merging as "neuropsychology." However, these researchers were not clinicians because they did not work with patients directly. Their tests were typically used to assess behavior in healthy people, not those with illnesses. Some of the first clinical measures can be credited to the research laboratory of Ward Halstead and Ralph Reitan.

Like his peers, Ward Halstead was an experimental psychologist who studied the behavior of animals. He paired with Ralph Reitan, a clinical psychologist who maintained a patient-oriented outlook towards brain functioning. This unique pairing of an experimentalist and a clinical psychologist in part allowed for the development of tests designed to detect abnormal brain function. Their intent was primarily to detect suspected brain lesions in patients with strokes, tumors, head injuries, and similar brain diseases. In this sense, they were successful. By taking the established science of behavioral neurology and standardizing human performance on a selected group of measures, they were able to develop a set battery that identified and tracked lesions quite accurately for that time period (see footnote 2).

In further exploring how neuropsychology evolved, it is worth reviewing two distinct fields that Halstead, Reitan, and others have merged into what we can now consider to be the field of modern neuropsychology: behavioral neurology and psychological testing.

Behavioral Neurology

Behavioral neurology is the study of the impact that damage to the brain has on behavior and cognition. In this sense it overlaps with neuropsychology, although behavioral neurology is a medical specialty while neuropsychology stems from psychology. Modern behavioral neurologists and neuropsychologists owe much of their respective fields to the same researchers who established localization of brain functioning and behavior, such as the aphasia (loss of language) work by Broca and Carl Wernicke.

Perhaps the most mechanistic illustration of functioning can be observed with the spinal cord. As the spinal cord is primarily concerned with motoric output and sensory input, damage along different levels can lead to predictable outcomes. Motoric and sensory dysfunction can therefore be identified to a remarkable degree of specificity. Sometimes the source of such dysfunction stems directly from the brain, either due to damage directly within the brain cortex, or due to the associated white matter tracts (i.e. "nerves" within the brain). Individuals trained in behavioral neurology are able to recognize the nature, course, and treatment options of numerous neurological conditions and, as mentioned, can identify damaged regions quite accurately. "Higher" aspects of human behavior, such as memory, attention, and language, can also be assessed and treated.

One cannot discuss these higher cognitive functions and their relationship to the brain without first mentioning Alexander Luria, another one of the founding fathers of neuropsychology, and particularly, child neuropsychology. Luria was a Soviet psychologist who was fascinated with the functional impact of brain dysfunction. Among many accomplishments, Luria was noted for his interest in the intersection between the biological state of the brain and the environment, specifically in relation to the cultural environment. For example, he observed how changes in perception and cognition could be directly linked with historical changes in economics and educational systems in various countries.

Although a neuropsychologist, Luria's work was closely linked with behavioral neurology. Much of his research focused on linguistic aphasia and he carried forward the understanding of the regional specificity associated with the language centers of the brain. He also studied the frontal lobes. Luria was among the first neuropsychologists to formally publish on the functional organization of the central nervous system, and the idea that different brain areas must work effectively in concert to result in "normal" human behavior. His work has undoubtedly influenced how neuroscientists today envision the central nervous system.

Luria's theories were later adapted into neuropsychological measures, such as the Luria-Nebraska battery. It differed somewhat from other batteries at the time in that it placed an emphasis on behavioral observations of brain dysfunction (e.g. left/right differences in the visual fields). Such techniques are quite similar to the approaches used by behavioral neurologists conducting a basic exam and reflects the debt that neuropsychological assessment owes towards this field.

Some critics of the Luria-Nebraska battery point out that this battery focuses too much on qualitative observations of behavior. Whether or not such criticism is valid, it highlights another discipline inherent to neuropsychological assessment – that of psychometrics.

Psychological Testing

Psychological testing (i.e. psychometrics) is another key aspect of psychology. You would be hard pressed to find a single psychologist who has not had any experience with psychological testing. In fact, it is one of the defining services provided by psychologists. Neuropsychologists have adapted a number of tests for their batteries, some of which are similar (if not identical) to those administered by other psychologists and others that are more unique.

As researchers in the 19th and 20th century studied human behavior, it was only natural that measures of such behavior would be used and eventually taken outside of the laboratory.

Alfred Binet developed what might be considered the first intelligence test. The Binet-Simon scale was the result of a request for Binet to develop a test designed to evaluate children prior to school admissions (see footnote 3). Questions ranged from sensory tasks (e.g. talking to the examiner), to identifying body parts, to drawing images from memory, to repeating digits back to the examiner, to answering logic puzzles. Binet's innovations proved so effective that many of these features are still used in tests today.

In the United States, World War I had sparked a call for additional testing to determine the mental fitness of enlisted men, resulting in the development of the *Army Alpha* and *Army Beta* tests, aspects of which remain in use today. The end of WWI led to golden era of psychological testing, with numerous intelligence, cognitive, and personality tests emerging in the United States. The desire to measure and predict human functioning based on psychometric evidence was prominent everywhere. David Wechsler was standardizing his first Wechsler scale, the Wechsler-Bellevue (supposedly on people on the beach at Coney Island) and his methods of employing standardized scores and objective norms set an unprecedented level of psychometric sophistication towards psychology tests.

It was within this environment where Halstead and Reitan found enormous success with their work. They believed that "biological intelligence" could best be evaluated by quantitative indicators and were particularly interested in differences in quantitative performance among distinct neurological populations. Together they amassed a repertoire of data examining discrepancies in performance among these groups. Of note, they incorporated the Wechsler-Bellevue intelligence scale into their battery, perhaps initiating the now traditional inclusion of IQ batteries in a neuropsychological assessment.

The most common method of identifying impairment is through the normative method that was widely used by Wechsler's group. This method is completed by administering a specific test to so-called "normal" individuals of a certain age group and sometimes, of a specific educational level or other demographics. Patients' scores are then compared to this normal group and a standard score, with an associated percentile, is obtained.

For example, a ten- year old boy is suspected of having a learning disability. A psychologist (or neuropsychologist) might administer a test that measures attention. The child successfully answers a certain number of items right – let's say he scored five out of a possible twelve answers. These five points sum into a raw score that is then compared to other ten year olds. Perhaps this subtest was administered previously to 300 "typical" boys and girls and the average score of this group was seven. Along with an average score, one has to consider the average deviation, or *standard deviation*, from the mean score. Based on the normative population's mean and standard deviation, you can make inferences on how unusual this particular children's raw score of five is from other ten year olds.

This only scratches the surface of psychometrics and interested readers will find additional detail in Chapter 3, particularly in how neuropsychologists might interpret the data of your child. Regardless, it is important to note that standard scores and percentiles are the most common and useful method of quantifiably identifying abnormalities (and exceptionalities) in children and adults.

Towards Functional Assessment

Up until the 1970's, neuropsychological assessment was one of the most effective ways to detect and pinpoint neurological injury. Advances in neuroimaging (CT and MRI scans) allowed clinicians to see the brain with greater accuracy. Some professionals predicted that scans would eventually replace the need for neuropsychological assessment, although this proved premature. While scans can detect injury, they cannot assess functional ability to the degree that neuropsychological assessment can. Better functional assessment became the focus of research efforts in the field of neuropsychology.

A group in Boston led by Edith Kaplan had already developed additional methods of assessment. She and her collaborators eschewed the fixed-battery approach of the Halstead–Reitan test and were less concerned with quantitative scores. While psychometrically validated tests were still important, they in of themselves were not considered to be the final word on clinical interpretation. Her laboratory stressed the importance of examining the methods by which patients approached tests alongside the summary scores. This qualitative, "process approach" allowed for more flexible batteries tailored to patients' needs and addresses the fact that numerous mental and behavioral strategies may ultimately lead to the same score on a test, yet indicate vastly different approaches (see footnote 4).

Groups all over the country began developing and improving on measures and how they best capture functional capacity and outcome. By "capacity" and "outcome" I refer to one's potential to carry out a task, and then whether that potential is actually used in the real world. These terms gained increasing relevance in neuropsychological assessment as there was a real need to establish that performance on neuropsychological measures actually translated towards meaningful outcomes. Thousands of studies were generated that established the *predictive validity* of tests, ultimately establishing that the right combination of tests and methodology did indeed yield relevant information about a patient. Perhaps most pertinent to the reader is the method in which such tests were used to predict a child's potential, both inside and outside of the classroom.

History of Pediatric/Child Neuropsychology

Pediatric/child neuropsychology is a recent discipline that is rooted in adult neuropsychology and pediatric neurology. If adult neuropsychology is considered to be the study of brain-behavior relationships, then pediatric neuropsychology can be viewed as this study within a developing human being. Although pediatric neuropsychology as a specific discipline was not established until the 1980s, neurodevelopmental disorders were observed and recorded by Hippocrates as far back as 400 BCE. In the 19th century, a team of neurologists and pediatricians merged these two disciplines into pediatric neurology. As mentioned, Luria was very fascinated with the developmental aspects of the human brain and included children in many of his studies. Later pioneers included Barbara Wilson, who began to classify and assess learning disorders and pervasive developmental disorders, and Byron Rourke, who had an interest in applying the Halstead–Reitan battery towards children.

By the 1970s, several children's batteries had emerged. Alongside these batteries came an increased interest in the specific field of pediatric neuropsychology. The initial assumption was that adult approaches of assessing cognition could be used with children. This assumption was based on the false premise that child disorders are as static as adult disorders. For example, brain injury in adults may lead to predictable lateralized deficits (e.g. injury in the right hemisphere might impede certain visual–spatial functions). However, in children the connectivity among brain regions is continuously evolving, and so such general assumptions can no longer be applied. In addition, neurologic injury in an adult often leads to a loss of functioning, while a similar injury may simply inhibit the ability for the function to even develop (see footnote 5).

A great deal of emphasis was placed on learning disorders. In the 1970s and 1980s, such disorders were often diagnosed although clinicians often had little understanding of their cause. The predominant method of diagnosis was to look at discrepancies between IQ test scores and academic achievement batteries. Unfortunately, by focusing solely on the psychometric scores of the tests, clinicians often neglected other contributing factors including the child's environment and family, emotional/personality issues, and underlying disruption to the central nervous system. The latter point has sparked some debate on whether learning disabilities can truly be classified as a medical/neurological condition, or whether they are simply a descriptor of some kind of behavioral and academic delay that could have any number of causes.

Official Guidelines

Pediatric neuropsychology was firmly established alongside adult neuropsychology in 1987, when a joint task force of neuropsychologists developed the first formal guidelines of clinical neuropsychology. Prior to 1987, there were several practitioners who referred to themselves as neuropsychologists but no training guidelines were firmly established. Therefore, anyone who decided to practice neuropsychology could do so with minimal oversight other than personal reputation. The formal guidelines, called the Houston guidelines, set out a specific path towards competency that is now almost universally followed today. Chapter 2 provides more detail on how you might ensure that a neuropsychologist follows these guidelines, which is an important step in choosing your practitioner.

With the formation of the Houston guidelines there came a plethora of training programs at the graduate, intern, and post-doctoral level. Today new programs are developing across the country as more and more neuropsychologists enter the workforce. Such programs generally follow the Houston guidelines and provide comprehensive training, usually first in general psychological methods including assessment and therapy at the graduate level, with specialization in neuropsychological methods at the intern and post-doctoral level. There are several societies for neuropsychologists including the International Neuropsychological Society (INS), the National Academy of Neuropsychology (NAN), and the American Academy of Clinical Neuropsychology (AACN). Board certification in neuropsychology is now considered an important step by many as it guarantees that a practitioner has satisfactorily met all the criteria of the Houston guidelines. This final step in a neuropsychologist's training only occurs after the post-doctoral level (usual after 1–5 years of working in the field) and is overseen by the American Board of Clinical Neuropsychology (ABCN).

State of Neuropsychology

Despite its young status, neuropsychology is a rapidly developing field. Neuropsychologists are employed in hospitals (inpatient and outpatient), academic medical centers, psychology departments, mental health clinics, schools, and private practices. Neuropsychologists are used to assess individuals with known brain dysfunction (e.g. stroke, brain injury) as well as suspected illness (e.g. dementia). They are called upon in forensic settings to evaluate cognitive and emotional changes in examinees, and continue to conduct research on under- lying causes of neurological and psychiatric illnesses.

Pediatric neuropsychologists generally fit in one of two groups, although there is substantial overlap between these groups. Some pediatric neuropsychologists focus primarily on learning and neuro- developmental disorders and often work with children with learning disabilities, ADHD, communication disorders, and autistic spec- trum disorders. The second group focus more on children who are serviced in a hospital or similar setting and see cases with brain injury, seizure disorder, brain tumors, and other neurological diseases. This division is somewhat arbitrary as both groups are typically trained to work with the other populations as part of their training and some neuropsychologists work with children presenting with any and all conditions; indeed, there are lifespan neuropsychologists (such as this author) who have had training with children and adults of all ages.

The current state of neuropsychology has moved from its primarily diagnostic roots towards a more functional and multidis- ciplinary approach. Pediatric neuropsychologists are often part of a treatment team involving educational therapists, other psycholo- gists, medical doctors, and schools to help children overcome their deficits, either through direct treatment or through compensatory strategies. Neuropsychologists also often serve as "lynchpins" of such teams, as they are familiar with the language and culture of various professions and can assist in effective communication among groups. Furthermore, neuropsychologists, like many Ph.D. level psycholo- gists, are trained in research methods and many are able to evaluate the efficacy of evidence-based interventions.

Neuropsychology has and continues to be an evolving field. The combination of psychology and neurology allows neuropsychologists to flexibly fit in a number of different settings. In fact, there are some exciting new opportunities for aspiring neuropsychologists that may emerge in the next decade (see footnote 6). Maybe more importantly, this discipline is now firmly entrenched in the medical, psychological, and educational fields and its practitioners can provide a unique service for you and your children.

FOOTNOTE 1

Paul Broca was a pioneer in *cortical localization*, or the theory that specific regions of the brain controlled distinct behavior functions across people. A French surgeon, he encountered a patient who could only speak in repetitive syllables, despite understanding everything that was said to him. Upon the patient's death, Broca conducted an autopsy and saw significant damage to the left side of the frontal lobe. This region, now called Broca's region, is recognized to be a critical area for the production of speech in adults. Of note, modern neuroanatomy has established that *cortical networks*, rather than specific regions, better explain the complexity of human behavior. However, Broca's area and the associated Wernicke's area remain two well-established examples of localized specificity.

FOOTNOTE 2

The Halstead-Reitan battery is composed of tests that assess attention, sensory perception, visual-spatial functioning, motor skills, language, and executive functions. One test examined how fast a patient tapped their index finger on a counting device. Another test had patients hold objects (e.g. cross, triangle) in their hands through a curtain and ascertain the shape through tactile sensation alone. Yet another test had patients look at images and decide which number (ranging 1-4) best captured that image. These tests varied immensely in administration and modality and captured a number of basic human behaviors. The battery also was designed to assess both the level of overall performance, pattern discrepancies among subtests, and sides of lateralized impairment in the right or left hemispheres. A fourth consideration, the observation of pathnomognic signs of neurological illness, was also a key aspect of the Halstead-Reitan battery.

FOOTNOTE 3

Binet's methods of standardizing scores are somewhat crude compared to modern methods but nonetheless innovative for its time. Binet identified tests that his group believed represented what children could do at certain ages. His group then took fifty children who were identified as "average" and observed how well they could do these tests. These "average" children served as the first standardization sample. Children undergoing assessment were measured based on the mental age of the test; therefore, children who were seven years of age who could pass tests designed for seven-year-olds were considered average. Those who underperformed had lower mental ages while those who performed better had higher mental ages.

FOOTNOTE 4

The process approach acknowledges the fact that many different thought processes and behaviors can ultimately come to the same score on a test. Take the example of a simple puzzle test in which a child has to put together blocks to match an image in a book. One child might recognize the individual parts that make up the image and arrange each block piece by piece to put it together. Another child might "get" the overall image and immediately piece together the blocks without much focus on individual parts. Either child might jump immediately into the task without little thought, or hesitate and take their time to ensure they are correct. It might even be possible to verbalize what the image looks like, circumnavigating the "purely" nonverbal nature of the test. Regardless of the processes involved, the examiner would still give points for successful completion (perhaps weighted by speed) and assign a "0" for either unsuccessfully matching the image, or taking too long to match it. In the process approach, the examiner would take care in accounting for as many factors as possible through behavioral observations, which factor in as much (if not more) than actual test scores in clinical decision-making.

FOOTNOTE 5

The *crowding* hypothesis, first introduced by Paul Satz, provides a nice illustration of the functional differences between children and adults. While adults with lesions to Broca's area might lose the ability to verbally express themselves, young children often develop normal language even when the same region is damaged. Pediatric neurology has established that the language center of the brain simply shifts to the opposite (typically right) hemisphere in the face of damage, perhaps due to the crucial importance of language development in humans. Satz's crowding hypothesis posits that when this shift occurs, it comes at a cost of other cognitive functions; for example, visual-spatial impairments are often present in children with left hemisphere lesions. This is because the right hemisphere, which often handles visual-spatial functions, is compromised in its need to handle the language network.

FOOTNOTE 6

Neuropsychologists are increasingly called upon to assist with neuroimaging, particularly functional neuroimaging. Structural neuroimaging (e.g. CT and MRI scans) look at a static picture of the brain in the context of identifying neurological illnesses and brain damage. In contrast, functional neuroimaging allows for a dynamic look at the change of blood flow, electric activity, and other functional representations of cortical activity. One notable role of the neuropsychologist is to establish language functioning in patients who are brought in for surgical resection (e.g. due to epilepsy), in order to ensure that important part of the brain's language center is not unnecessarily removed. A combination of Wada testing (a localized cortical anesthetic), behavioral testing, and functional neuroimaging can allow for unprecedented specificity in identifying parts of the brain that are vital for language.

Bibliography

Barkley, R. A. (2013). *Taking charge of ADHD: The complete, authoritative guide for parents*. Guilford press.

Blumenfeld, H. (2010). *Neuroanatomy through clinical cases*. Sinauer Associates.

Davis, A. S., & D'Amato, R. C. (Eds.). (2010). *Handbook of pediatric neuropsychology*. Springer Publishing Company.

Kaufman, D. M. (2007). *Clinical neurology for psychiatrists*. Elsevier Health Sciences.

Reynolds, C., & Fletcher-Janzen, E. (2013). *Handbook of clinical child neuropsychology*. Springer.

Schoenberg, M. R., & Scott, J. G. (Eds.). (2011). *The little black book of neuropsychology: a syndrome-based approach*. Springer Science & Business Media.

Semrud-Clikeman, M., & Ellison, P. A. T. (2009). *Child neuropsychology: Assessment and interventions for neurodevelopmental disorders*. Springer Science & Business Media.

About the Author

Nicholas S. Thaler, Ph.D., is a licensed clinical neuropsychologist who conducts neuropsychological evaluations across the lifespan. He obtained his Ph.D. at the University of Nevada, Las Vegas where he specialized in child neuropsychology, completed his internship at the University of Oklahoma Health Sciences Center, and finished a two-year post-doctoral fellowship at the UCLA Semel Institute for Neuroscience & Human Behavior where he obtained experience with adults. He has published over 50 papers examining the cognitive and psychiatric sequelae of a number of clinical conditions across the lifespan including learning disabilities, ADHD, pediatric traumatic brain injury, HIV, and bipolar disorder. He has worked at children's hospitals, academic medical centers, child community centers, private practices, and a Veteran's Affairs hospital. He specializes in assessing learning disabilities, ADHD, and cognitive dysfunction secondary to medical injuries. Dr. Thaler has been recognized with a number of accolades, including the Tony Wong Diversity Award, the Nevada Regent's Scholar Award, the UNLV President's Scholarship, and a UCLA Center for AIDS Research seed grant. He maintains a private practice in Los Angeles, California where he lives with his wife, son, and dog. If you would like to learn more about Dr. Thaler and his practice, please visit *www.nicholasthaler.com*.

CPSIA information can be obtained
at www.ICGtesting.com
Printed in the USA
FSHW021008170821
84127FS

9 781536 973822